THE DYNAMICS OF WORK
Student Supplement

WILLARD R. DAGGETT, PRESIDENT
INTERNATIONAL CENTER FOR LEADERSHIP & DEVELOPMENT
Schenectady, New York

JAMES E. MILES, CHAIRPERSON
Business Education Department
Pittsford Sutherland High School
Pittsford, New York

Update to the Second Edition

JOIN US ON THE INTERNET
WWW: http://www.thomson.com
EMAIL: findit@kiosk.thomson.com   A service of I T P®

South-Western
Educational Publishing

South-Western Educational Publishing
an International Thomson Publishing company I T P®

Cincinnati ●Albany, NY ● Belmont, CA ● Bonn ● Boston ● Detroit ● Johannesburg ● London ● Madrid
Melbourne ● Mexico City ● New York ● Paris ● Singapore ● Tokyo ● Toronto ● Washington

4 5 6 7 8 9 PN 05 04 03 02 01

Printed in the United States of America

CONTENTS

INTRODUCTION

This student supplement is an applications workbook that supplements and complements *The Dynamics of Work* textbook. The workbook provides an opportunity for you to apply the information learned from the textbook and in the classroom in a variety of ways.

Each of the 29 chapters in this supplement includes at least three and often all five of the following applications:

- **Vocabulary Practice.** Each of the chapters includes a vocabulary exercise. The type of exercise varies from chapter to chapter but may consist of matching, fill in the blanks, crossword puzzles, or sentence definitions.
- **Short Answer Questions.** Many chapters contain one or more short answer exercises. You are to answer each question in an exercise using one or two complete sentences.
- **Sentence Completion.** In each of these exercises, you are to match a list of terms to the blanks in a series of sentences. Be alert. In some exercises, there are more terms from which to choose than there are blanks to be filled.
- **Cases.** Most of the chapters contain at least one short case. You are to read the scenario and answer the questions that follow it. Again, use complete sentences in your answers.
- **Put Yourself in the Picture.** In these exercises you will relate your personal life situations to the material you have studied in the textbook.

Helping you understand your future role as a working citizen is the primary goal of *The Dynamics of Work* textbook. This student supplement is designed to assure your learning achievement.

YOU
AND
BUSINESS

VOCABULARY PRACTICE

Directions: Match the terms in Column *B* with the phrases in Column *A* by writing the letter of the term next to the phrase that best describes that term.

Column A

_____ 1. A person who works for someone else, usually for wages or salary.

_____ 2. An activity that provides for the wants and needs of a person, group, or organization.

_____ 3. A set rate of payment to an employee, usually on a weekly or monthly basis.

_____ 4. Something that must be done, completed, or paid, according to a previous agreement

_____ 5. A need or want, especially for goods or services.

_____ 6. Committed to a person.

_____ 7. A person or business that provides or creates jobs for other people.

_____ 8. An action that benefits others.

_____ 9. Physical items for sale; merchandise.

_____ 10. A binding agreement between two or more parties.

_____ 11. Without any job-related training or special abilities.

_____ 12. A measurement of the rate of output toward or contribution to the opertation of a business.

_____ 13. Something of value that is offered for sale by a business.

_____ 14. Having to answer for one's own conduct or obligations.

_____ 15. A person who observes and directs the work of others.

Column B

A. business

B. customer

C. demand

D. resource

E. employer

F. employee

G. contract

H. obligation

I. supervisor

J. wage

K. salary

L. prejudice

M. favoritism

N. loyal

O. product

P. service

Q. goods

R. productivity

S. responsibility

T. unskilled

U. career

V. profession

SHORT ANSWER QUESTIONS

Directions: Use your textbook, *The Dynamics of Work,* and your own personal experiences to answer each question in complete sentences.

1. Why is a job considered a continuing business transaction?

_____

_____

_____

2. As a worker, what would you consider fair treatment by your employer?

_____

_____

_____

3. How does a worker demonstrate loyalty to an employer?

_____

_____

_____

4. Which two job satisfiers do you consider most important and why?

_____

_____

_____

5. Which two employer satisfiers do you feel will be easiest for you to fulfill and why?

_____

_____

_____

_____

CHAPTER 1 • YOU AND BUSINESS

SENTENCE COMPLETION

Directions: Using the list below, select the term that best completes each statement. No term is to be used more than once.

product	goods
supervision	careers
professionals	productivity
unskilled	responsibility
demand	employer
service	favoritism

1. An obligation is a _____ .

2. Your value to an employer depends largely upon your _____ .

. _____ is what a business sells.

   A barber or cosmetologist sells a _____ .

5. An _____ should provide _____

   _____ for employees.

6. Many people are considered _____ workers when

   they begin their _____ .

7. Individuals whose careers require special knowledge and schooling are called _____

   _____ .

8. _____ by an employer is unfair to workers.

9. _____ are physical items for sale.

PUT YOURSELF IN THE PICTURE

Directions: Write a brief statement relating this chapter, "You and Business," to your everyday life. Choose a parent or guardian and describe how this person earns a living. Explain how this affects you.

_____

_____

_____

_____

_____

_____

_____

_____

_____

_____

_____

_____

_____

CHAPTER 1 • YOU AND BUSINESS

DYNAMICS AT WORK

Directions: Read the following case carefully. Answer the questions using the information in the case and in Chapter 1.

Lisa placed her lunch tray on the table and waved to Connie, who was nearing the end of the cafeteria line. Lisa could hardly wait to tell her friend the good news.

As Connie put her tray down, she sensed that Lisa was excited. "You look as if you're dying to tell me something," Connie said.

"I sure am!" Lisa said. "I just got a big promotion at work. Now I won't have to go job hunting after graduation."

"That's great," Connie said. "What happened?"

"My boss, Mr. Andersen, asked me yesterday if I'd like to work full time when school's over. He said I was doing very well on correspondence. I'm sure glad I took that computer awareness course last semester. Mr. Andersen said he was impressed with my ability to use the word processing equipment. Apparently, no one else in the office has made much progress with it so far. He even complimented me on my spelling and grammar, of all things," Lisa said, shaking her head.

"It sounds like you're making real progress," Connie said.

"I'm excited about it. Mr. Andersen is going to pay me another dollar an hour when I start full-time work. He also told me that he wants me to learn all about credit and billing. The credit manager is planning to retire next year. If I can learn fast enough, I'll get that job. That would mean a really big raise," Lisa said.

"That's great for someone just starting out in the world of work," Connie said. "It's especially nice because you like the people there."

"Yes," Lisa said. "It's true that there is more to work than just collecting a salary."

1. In what specific ways did Lisa impress Mr. Andersen with her productivity?

_____

_____

_____

_____

2. List the rungs Lisa has taken and those she has planned to take in her career ladder.

_____

_____

_____

_____

3. What are the employee satisfiers Lisa has on her job?

_____

_____

_____

_____

THE
BUSINESS
SYSTEM

VOCABULARY PRACTICE

Directions: Match the terms in Column *B* with the phrases in Column *A* by writing the letter of the term next to the phrase that best describes that term.

Column A

_____ 1. Engaging in a transaction.

_____ 2. An exchange of values.

_____ 3. The owner of a business.

_____ 4. A skilled worker who has completed a training period; the skill level immediately above an apprentice.

_____ 5. To purchase full or partial ownership in an entity in exchange for some value such as money.

_____ 6. To form a continuous, cyclical flow of money, or other things commonly held as valuable, through a system.

_____ 7. A chance that something might lead to gain or to loss.

_____ 8. A field of skilled labor.

_____ 9. A person who is learning an art or skill on the job.

_____ 10. A person or organization wanting to fulfill a need by making a purchase.

Column B

A. risk

B. buyer

C. transaction

D. invest

E. doing business

F. trade

G. journeyman

H. proprietor

I. apprentice

J. circulate

K. seller

L. threshold

SHORT ANSWER QUESTIONS

Directions: Use your textbook, *The Dynamics of Work,* and your own personal experiences to answer each question in complete sentences.

1. Describe two ways in which business affects your daily life.

_____

_____

_____

2. Why is time an important consideration in your business dealings?

_____

_____

_____

3. How does a business circulate money in a community?

_____

_____

_____

4. Why does the investment of resources create a risk?

_____

_____

_____

5. What kinds of investments will you have to make to increase your value as a working citizen?

_____

_____

_____

_____

CHAPTER 2 • THE BUSINESS SYSTEM

SENTENCE COMPLETION

Directions: Using the list below, select the term that best completes each statement. No term is to be used more than once.

invests	demand
journeyman	trade
seller	customers
buyer	transaction
circulate	risk
apprentice	proprietor

1. _____ purchase the goods or services offered by a business.

2. The _____ carpenter learns job skills from a

_____ .

3. Buying a hamburger is a business _____ .

4. A business owner _____ resources in a business.

5. If you want to purchase a new pair of designer jeans, you have created a _____

_____ .

6. Businesses help to _____ money in a community.

7. A business _____ takes a _____
by investing money and effort.

8. A customer of a business is a _____ of the goods or
services offered by that business.

PUT YOURSELF IN THE PICTURE

Directions: Write a brief statement relating this chapter, "The Business System," to your everyday life. Explain your role as a customer, or buyer, of products. How do you, as a consumer, affect the business life of your community?

_____

_____

_____

_____

_____

_____

_____

_____

_____

_____

_____

_____

_____

_____

_____

CHAPTER 2 • THE BUSINESS SYSTEM

DYNAMICS AT WORK

Directions: Read the following case carefully. Answer the questions using the information in the case and in Chapter 2.

His parents had given Todd a choice when they left for the theater. He could stay at home and cook whatever he felt like eating, or he could walk down to the Diamond Cafe for a roast beef sandwich. His father had given him $5 in case he chose the roast beef sandwich.

Todd looked in the refrigerator. Nothing there appealed to him at that moment. Maybe it was because he really didn't feel like cooking anyway. Besides, he was sure he'd see his friend David at the Diamond Cafe. He decided to eat out.

Todd didn't bother to read the menu on the wall behind the serving counter. He ordered what he wanted as soon as he arrived. "I'll have a roast beef sandwich and a large milk." The cashier totaled the order. It came to $3.85. Todd paid the bill and got his receipt. He looked around the dining area. David was sitting in a booth near the back.

"I'm glad you're here," Todd said. "We have to decide what to take on that field trip."

"No problem," David replied. "I wrote down a list. Take a look and tell me what you think."

Todd nodded in agreement. "Looks okay to me," he said. Just then, his order number was called over the loudspeaker.

Todd enjoyed his roast beef sandwich. "They really have their act together here, don't they, David?"

"They make the best roast beef sandwiches in town," David agreed.

"They also make pretty good money, considering the price of roast beef. A pound of roast beef was $4.80 in the market today. My sandwich had about one sixth of a pound of meat and cost $3. That means they bring in $3 for $.80 worth of meat. That would be a huge profit margin if meat were the only cost factor," Todd said. "I wonder what they really make on a sandwich."

"Well, there are quite a few costs involved in this business," David said. "They have to buy rolls, lettuce, tomatoes, salad dressing—anything you might want on your sandwich."

"Right," Todd agreed. "And they buy napkins, plates and cups, wrapping paper, and all sorts of supplies. They have to pay for the cooks, cashiers, and counter persons, too."

"Don't forget the rent on the building," David added. "You've seen that little crafts shop my Mom operates. She pays $600 a month to rent that space. On top of that, this place probably has some heavy bills for electricity and gas."

"A business has to have insurance, too," Todd said. "With all those costs, a person running a business has to be pretty smart to make a good living. I guess it helps to enjoy your work."

1. A transaction involves an exchange of things of value. What were the values exchanged between Todd and the Diamond Cafe? Be specific.

_____

_____

_____

_____

_____

_____

2. How do the costs of running the Diamond Cafe help to circulate money in the community? List five specific ways this is done.

_____

_____

_____

_____

_____

_____

3. Did the values Todd received satisfy his wants? Be specific; list Todd's wants in one column and the value that satisfied each want in another column.

_____

_____

_____

_____

_____

_____

EMPLOYMENT:
SELECTING
YOUR
COURSE

VOCABULARY PRACTICE

Directions: Match the terms in Column *B* with the phrases in Column *A* by writing the letter of the term next to the phrase that best describes that term.

Column A

_____ 1. A person's value, or worth, as seen by others.

_____ 2. The effect or result of an action or decision.

_____ 3. A person's manner of living.

_____ 4. That which a person is capable of becoming.

_____ 5. A written presentation that covers a person's background and experiences.

_____ 6. A non-necessity that is desired for the feeling of satisfaction it will provide.

_____ 7. An organized way of working toward a planned result.

_____ 8. A good or service that is required for the well-being of a person or organization.

Column B

A. consequence
B. personal profile
C. self-esteem
D. process approach
E. potential
F. need
G. esteem
H. want
I. solitude
J. lifestyle

SHORT ANSWER QUESTIONS

Directions: Use your textbook, *The Dynamics of Work,* and your own personal experiences to answer each question in complete sentences.

1. Why is the process approach valuable in selecting a career?

_____

_____

_____

_____

2. What steps are involved in developing your personal profile?

_____

_____

_____

_____

3. Which of your characteristics will you examine in considering possible career choices?

_____

_____

_____

4. What is meant by the statement that "aptitudes will increase in value as you build skills and knowledge around them"?

_____

_____

_____

5. What is meant by the statement that the "world of work is dynamic"?

_____

_____

_____

CHAPTER 3 • EMPLOYMENT: SELECTING YOUR COURSE

SENTENCE COMPLETION

Directions: Using the list below, select the term that best completes each statement. No term is to be used more than once.

process approach	personality
potential	punctual
consequence	self-esteem
aptitude	decision
enterprising	lifestyle
solitude	esteem

1. An _____ worker is also usually _____

   _____ .

2. Using a _____ is often the best method of making

   a _____ .

3. The _____ you want is a consideration in making
   a career choice.

4. The way others see you is a measure of your _____ .

5. _____ is your worth as you determine it.

6. Your _____ is everything you are capable of becoming.

7. The ability to work with mathematics is an _____ .

8. Strengths and weaknesses involve your body, your mind, and your _____ _____

   _____ .

DYNAMICS AT WORK

Directions: Read the following case carefully. Answer the questions using the information in the case and in Chapter 3.

Heidi put away her schoolwork and went downstairs to the living room, where her father was reading the evening newspaper. "May I borrow the classified ad section of your paper, Dad?" she asked.

"Sure, honey. Are you looking for anything in particular?" her father asked.

"I want to look through the help-wanted ads to see what's available. I'd like to get a full-time job for the summer, and I thought I'd get an early start," Heidi said.

"That's fine," her father said. "What kind of work do you want?"

"I'm not really sure, Dad. That's why I'm starting to look well ahead of time. I think I'd like retail sales," Heidi said.

Her father handed Heidi the classified ad pages. "It's fine to check on the job situation, but you shouldn't make any hasty decisions. Do your homework first," he said.

"What do you mean, Dad?" Heidi asked.

"Think about your strengths and weaknesses. Write them down. Consider what kinds of work you would enjoy. Get to know yourself a little better, and look for a job that matches your abilities and interests," her father said.

"That makes sense," Heidi said. "Even if it's just a summer job, I want to do my best. The classified ads can wait until I have a better idea of the kind of job for which I'm best suited."

1. What steps should Heidi take before she looks through the classified ads?

_____

_____

_____

_____

2. What did Heidi's father mean when he said "get to know yourself a little better"?

_____

_____

_____

_____

CHAPTER 3 • EMPLOYMENT: SELECTING YOUR COURSE

PUT YOURSELF IN THE PICTURE

Directions: Write a brief statement relating this chapter, "Employment: Selecting Your Course," to your everyday life. Select a part-time job that interests you. Discuss the strengths and weaknesses you would bring to that job.

_____

_____

_____

_____

_____

_____

_____

_____

_____

_____

_____

_____

_____

_____

_____

_____

_____

_____

PREPARATION
FOR
EMPLOYMENT

VOCABULARY PRACTICE

Directions: Match the terms in Column *B* with the phrases in Column *A* by writing the letter of the term next to the phrase that best describes that term.

Column A	*Column B*
_____ 1. Moral standards.	A. attitudes
_____ 2. Reading, math, and language.	B. limitation
_____ 3. Types, models, or examples for comparison.	C. civil service
_____ 4. An attitude, value, or physical or mental factor that works against success on the job.	D. values
	E. life cycle
_____ 5. Most complete single reference guide for jobs and careers.	F. *Dictionary of Occupational Titles*
	G. basic academic skills
_____ 6. States of mind, behavior, or conduct regarding some matter.	H. standards

SHORT ANSWER QUESTIONS

Directions: Use your textbook, *The Dynamics of Work,* and your own personal experiences to answer each question in complete sentences.

1. What are the basic steps in the process of career planning?

_____

_____

_____

_____

2. List the print sources available to you for information about occupations.

_____

_____

_____

_____

3. List the nonprint sources available to you for information about occupations.

_____

_____

_____

4. How can your local telephone book help you to search for information about occupations?

_____

_____

_____

5. Explain the statement "Basic academic skills go hand in hand with basic skills having to do with values and attitudes."

_____

_____

_____

CHAPTER 4 • PREPARATION FOR EMPLOYMENT

SENTENCE COMPLETION

Directions: Using the list below, select the term that best completes each statement. No term is to be used more than once.

civil service   limitations
values   aspirations
attitude   life cycle
standards   basic skills

1. Employers expect and need certain _____ from workers.

2. Productivity and turning out quality work are _____ for what you do.

3. Your behavior in the workplace, along with your state of mind, make up your _____ .

4. Your _____ are part of your moral standards.

5. As you go through the _____ your goals will change.

6. Even though you may have the skills and aptitudes needed for a particular career area, you may have _____ that will prevent you from doing a good job.

PUT YOURSELF IN THE PICTURE

Directions: Write a brief statement relating this chapter, "Preparation for Employment," to your everyday life. Select a career that interests you. Match your aptitudes, interests, and lifestyle goals to the career area you selected.

_____

_____

_____

_____

_____

_____

_____

_____

_____

_____

_____

_____

_____

CHAPTER 4 • PREPARATION FOR EMPLOYMENT

PUTTING SOME MYTHS TO REST

Directions: Read the following paragraphs carefully. Answer the questions using the information below and in Chapter 4.

Misconceptions about work and career opportunities remain common in our society. Some critical misconceptions are corrected below:

Certain occupations are for men, while others are for women. You may select any career you desire, regardless of your sex. A girl may become a doctor, lawyer, plumber, or airline pilot. A boy may become a secretary, nursery school teacher, or nurse. Your sex should not be a primary consideration in evaluating your career targets.

Most people dislike their jobs. No one enjoys every single aspect of a job. Many individuals tend to talk about portions of their work or daily activities that they dislike. These negative comments occur because situations that bother people are uppermost in their minds. Things they like are accepted and are discussed less frequently. Therefore, you get the impression that they dislike their jobs, when in fact they are generally happy with them. Most people do not dislike their jobs. Those who do can change jobs if they desire to do so.

The more education I have, the greater amount of money I will make. There is often a relationship between a person's educational level and income. However, this relationship is frequently less meaningful than people believe. For example, workers in skilled trades are usually paid more than teachers who have at least four years of college. Education may increase your earning power, but it is not an assurance of higher income. Education typically provides a better background for selecting the kind of job that is of greatest interest to you. Education provides you with greater career flexibility.

All skills should be built in an educational setting. You are born with some skills; others are developed in educational settings; still others can be acquired on a job. No one should hope to gain all important skills in school. School is *one* source of skill development. Failure to use school to develop skills is a serious mistake. To develop your skills, you must do three things: (1) identify the skills you were born with, (2) develop those you can in school, and (3) continue developing them on the job.

Individuals are aware of skills they have. Most individuals have skills of which they are not aware. As a high-school student, you have not had an opportunity to test many skill areas that relate to jobs. Therefore, you may not be aware of your own skills. Most people have more skills than they realize. Only through experience and careful evaluations will you become aware of all the skills you possess.

Skills are not transferable to other jobs. Skills developed for one job can easily be transferred to another. Some skills relate to almost all occupations. Regardless of why a skill is developed, it may be used wherever it applies.

If a woman wishes to raise a family, she must postpone her career plans. Rearing children does not require a mother to leave the labor market for more than a brief time. A father can assume child care responsibilities, they can be shared by parents, or appropriate day care can be obtained. Raising a family should postpone a woman's career plans only if she so chooses.

1. Why do we have the impression that most people dislike their jobs?

_____

_____

_____

_____

2. If education does not guarantee that you will make more money, what benefit does it have?

_____

_____

_____

_____

3. What are the three things you must do to develop skills?

_____

_____

_____

_____

4. When should raising a family postpone a woman's career?

_____

_____

_____

_____

CHAPTER 6

**APPLYING
FOR
EMPLOYMENT**

VOCABULARY PRACTICE

Directions: Write a complete sentence defining each of the following terms.

1. application for employment

_____

_____

2. follow-up letter

_____

_____

3. classified ad

_____

_____

4. public utility company

_____

_____

5. labor union

_____

_____

6. union hall

_____

_____

SHORT ANSWER QUESTIONS

Directions: Use your textbook, *The Dynamics of Work,* and your own personal experiences to answer each question in complete sentences.

1. Why is it often best to submit a resume in advance of a job interview?

_____

_____

_____

2. In what circumstances should a letter of application accompany a resume?

_____

_____

_____

3. How could you occupy your time profitably while waiting for a job interview?

_____

_____

_____

4. If an interviewer offers to shake your hand, what should you do?

_____

_____

_____

5. What are the advantages to sending a follow-up letter after a job interview?

_____

_____

_____

CHAPTER 6 • APPLYING FOR EMPLOYMENT

SENTENCE COMPLETION

Directions: Using the list below, select the term that best completes each statement. No term is to be used more than once.

letter of application   job interview
follow-up letter   application for employment
classified ad   cover letter

1. When it accompanies a resume, a letter of application is also called a _____
   _____ .

2. In a _____ you can reinforce something you said in
   a job interview.

3. A _____ seeks to obtain a job interview.

4. An _____ is a form upon which an applicant lists
   qualifications for a job.

5. A _____ is an interview in which an employer
   evaluates a potential employee.

PUT YOURSELF IN THE PICTURE

Directions: Using the guidelines given in this chapter, "Applying for Employment," complete the following exercises based upon a classified ad you obtain from your local newspaper.

1. Compose a personal resume.

2. Write a letter of application for the advertised job, making sure you use the four paragraphs that should be included in such a letter.

3. Choose a company to which you would like to apply for a job, and tell how you would complete the basic steps that will help you prepare for an interview.

_____

_____

_____

_____

_____

_____

_____

_____

_____

_____

_____

_____

**GETTING
ALONG
AT WORK**

VOCABULARY PRACTICE

Directions: Write a complete sentence defining each of the following terms.

1. team

_____

_____

2. teamwork

_____

_____

3. organization

_____

_____

4. authority

_____

_____

5. responsibility

_____

_____

6. accountable

_____

_____

7. supervision

_____

_____

8. supervisor

_____

_____

9. policies

_____

_____

10. chain of command

_____

_____

11. rank

_____

_____

12. outrank

_____

_____

13. board of directors

_____

_____

14. reporting

_____

_____

15. formal reporting

_____

_____

CHAPTER 7 • GETTING ALONG AT WORK

16. informal reporting

_____

_____

17. organization chart

_____

_____

18. loyalty

_____

_____

19. grievance

_____

_____

20. management

_____

_____

21. strike

_____

_____

SHORT ANSWER QUESTIONS

Directions: Use your textbook, *The Dynamics of Work,* and your own personal experiences to answer each question in complete sentences.

1. What must you be willing to do to become a team player?

_____

_____

_____

_____

2. What are the two primary functions of a supervisor?

_____

_____

_____

3. Why is a chain of command important in any organization?

_____

_____

_____

_____

4. What is informal reporting?

_____

_____

_____

5. What is the proper method for initiating a grievance procedure?

_____

_____

_____

CHAPTER 7 • GETTING ALONG AT WORK

SENTENCE COMPLETION

Directions: Using the list below, select the term that best completes each statement. No term is to be used more than once.

organization chart	reporting
team	teamwork
policies	loyalty
authority	grievances
chain of command	management
rank	strike

1. A _____ is two or more people working together to produce the same results.

2. _____ are overall plans that state the goals and operating procedures of an organization.

3. _____ flows downward through a _____

_____ .

4. Answering to a higher ranking person is called_____ .

5. A visual presentation of a chain of command is called a(n) _____

_____ .

6. Major unresolved_____ on the job can lead to a

_____ .

7. _____ is a valued asset in a good employee.

8. The executive level of an organization is its _____ .

DYNAMICS AT WORK—CASE 1

Directions: Read the following case carefully. Answer the questions using the information in the case and in Chapter 7.

When Jeff heard the whistle, he looked over at the clock. It was exactly 4:30 p.m. His first day at work in the soft drink bottling plant was over.

Jeff pushed the button that stopped the conveyer belt carrying empty cases from the floor below. Unfortunately, he had found it necessary to press that button too often that first day. Whenever he failed to move fast enough, the cases would bunch up and the conveyer line would jam. He knew tomorrow would be better, though, because he had developed a good rhythm after a few hours.

Some of the other workers teased Jeff as they left the plant. "Hey, kid, do you think you can keep those cases moving tomorrow? We can't ship out one bottle at a time and make any money."

Jeff smiled. "Don't worry, you guys. When I get my rhythm going, you'll be fighting to keep up with me."

"That's the spirit, Jeff." The voice was that of his boss, Hank Brady. "You did pretty well today for your first day on the job. I'll show you a few more tricks tomorrow, and you'll be able to pick up your speed," Brady said.

When Jeff got home, he headed straight for the kitchen. "Hi, Mom. Your other working man is home," he said.

"Hello, Jeff. How was your first day at work?" his mother asked.

"Not bad at all," Jeff replied. "Actually, it was pretty nice. The other workers kid around a lot, but they all work hard. It's like being on a team. In fact, my boss, Mr. Brady, reminds me of Coach Robinson. He's a pretty good teacher, and he runs the team with a cool head. Just like Coach Robinson, he makes you want to do well. He seems like a good person to work for."

"I'm glad to hear you talk that way, son. You should do well if you have that team spirit. And, if you like the folks you work with, that's a real bonus," his mother said.

"Well, at least I think I'm off to a good start," Jeff said. "And I don't think it will take very long to become part of the team."

1. Why did Jeff compare Hank Brady to his coach in school?

_____

_____

_____

_____

2. Explain why Jeff's being able to pick up speed was important to the other workers.

_____

_____

_____

_____

3. Why do you think team spirit is important both at home and on the job?

_____

_____

_____

_____

4. How did Jeff show he wanted to become a member of the team at work?

_____

_____

_____

_____

DYNAMICS AT WORK—CASE 2

Directions: Read the following case carefully. Answer the questions using the information in the case and in Chapter 7.

Sue left her umbrella on the porch and shook the excess water from her raincoat before going inside. As she closed the front door, she heard her mother's voice from another room: "Is that you, Susan?"

"Yes, Mom, I'm home," Sue answered. She walked to the kitchen.

"How was everything at work, honey?" her mother asked, as Sue kissed her.

Sue checked to see what was cooking on the range. "It was pretty rough, Mom. They fired Richie today."

"Oh, that's a shame," her mother said. "What happened?"

"Well, Richie had been leaving work early some nights, and Ms. Jackson found out. One of the other salespersons complained that Richie had left her alone in the store a half-hour before closing. Suddenly, it got really busy, and she couldn't keep up with the customers. That cost the store some sales," Sue explained.

"That's not a good thing to do, but it doesn't seem like sufficient reason to fire someone," Sue's mother reflected.

"The trouble was that this was not the first time, Mom," Sue said. "Another girl said she had seen Richie at the coffee shop several times when he was supposed to be working. That convinced Ms. Jackson."

"Did anyone speak in Richie's defense?" Sue's mother asked.

"I did. I told Ms. Jackson how hard Richie usually works and how he helps the other salespersons when they need it," Sue said. "Richie wanted me to cover up for him, though, and I couldn't. I've known about his habit of leaving early for some time now, and I couldn't lie. The evidence was there. Besides, Ms. Jackson is a good manager and a fair boss. I felt I would be disloyal if I lied to her."

"You did the right thing, honey. I hope Richie doesn't blame you," Sue's mother said.

"I don't know. He was pretty upset when he left the store. We've been friends for a long time, though, and I think Richie realizes what he did was wrong. He'll come around," Sue said.

1. How did Sue display loyalty to Richie?

_____

_____

_____

_____

CHAPTER 7 • GETTING ALONG AT WORK

2. How did Sue display loyalty to her employer?

_____

_____

_____

3. Was Richie loyal to the store? Why?

_____

_____

_____

4. Was Richie loyal to his supervisor? Why?

_____

_____

_____

5. Was Richie loyal to other employees? Why?

_____

_____

_____

6. Was Richie loyal to Sue? Why?

_____

_____

_____

PUT YOURSELF IN THE PICTURE

Directions: Write a brief statement relating this chapter, "Getting Along at Work," to your everyday life. Describe a team or organization to which you belong or have belonged. Discuss your role in terms of authority, responsibility, and accountability.

_____

_____

_____

_____

_____

_____

_____

_____

_____

_____

_____

_____

_____

_____

_____

_____

_____

_____

_____

_____

YOUR
RIGHTS
AND
RESPONSIBILITIES
ON THE
JOB

VOCABULARY PRACTICE

Directions: Match the terms in Column *B* with the phrases in Column *A* by writing the letter of the term next to the phrase that best describes that term.

Column A

_____ 1. The least amount of money a worker may legally receive per hour.

_____ 2. Extra hours an employee works over the agreed upon number of regular hours per day or week.

_____ 3. Improper use or treatment.

_____ 4. A system providing those who are involuntarily out of work with compensation until a job can be found.

_____ 5. Insurance protection for workers hurt on the job.

_____ 6. A disagreement between workers and their employers.

_____ 7. Improper or immoral behavior.

_____ 8. Dishonest or deceitful.

_____ 9. Unfair treatment of a person or group of persons on the basis of traits or beliefs.

_____ 10. Soundness of body that enables one to work well on the job.

_____ 11. Soundness of mind that enables one to work well on the job.

_____ 12. Reasons given for failure to achieve an expected goal.

_____ 13. The ability to gain the cooperation of others.

_____ 14. People who are in a lower rank.

_____ 15. Negotiations between organized workers and their employers to come to some agreement about one or more issues.

Column B

A. subordinates

B. management

C. workers' compensation

D. self-control

E. minimum wage

F. abuse

G. collective bargaining

H. physical health

I. discrimination

J. performance evaluation

K. excuse

L. overtime

M. unemployment

N. misconduct

O. leadership

P. labor dispute

Q. fringe benefits

R. fraudulent

S. mental health

T. motivation

SHORT ANSWER QUESTIONS

Directions: Use your textbook, *The Dynamics of Work,* and your own personal experiences to answer each question in complete sentences.

1. Describe the type of management style under which you prefer to work.

_____

_____

_____

2. Explain why a person with a poor attitude is usually more unhappy than a person with a positive outlook on life.

_____

_____

_____

3. What are the three rules on which health and physical fitness depend?

_____

_____

_____

4. What types of discrimination are prohibited by federal law?

_____

_____

_____

5. Why are unemployment insurance and workers' compensation benefits important to workers?

_____

_____

_____

CHAPTER 8 • YOUR RIGHTS AND RESPONSIBILITIES ON THE JOB

SENTENCE COMPLETION

Directions: Using the list below, select the term that best completes each statement. No term is to be used more than once.

overtime	delegating	OSHA
excuse	fringe benefit	labor union
leadership	discrimination	motivation
collective bargaining	attitude	self-control
performance evaluations	seniority	subordinates
EEOC		

1. A good leader provides _____ to his or her subordinates.

2. Effective _____ generally results in effective management.

3. The agency that monitors and enforces safety rules and regulations is _____

_____ .

4. If a worker works 45 hours a week, he or she is usually paid _____

_____ for the hours worked over 40.

5. Refusing to hire someone because of age is called _____.

6. When a manager assigns one of his or her responsibilities to a subordinate, the manager

is _____ that responsibility.

7. A worker who is given a company car to drive is receiving a _____

_____ .

8. The _____ is the federal agency that guards against unfair labor practices.

9. Before a worker is fired, the worker should have received several _____

_____ .

10. Most people are better liked if they have a positive _____.

11. An effective leader will practice _____ so as not to show anger or frustration.

12. _____ must be done in good faith by both labor and management.

PUT YOURSELF IN THE PICTURE

Directions: Choose a job or a school activity in which you have been involved, and describe your rights and responsibilities in that activity. Use complete sentences and proper paragraphs.

_____

_____

_____

_____

_____

_____

_____

_____

_____

_____

_____

_____

_____

_____

_____

_____

_____

_____

CHAPTER 8 • YOUR RIGHTS AND RESPONSIBILITIES ON THE JOB

DYNAMICS AT WORK

Directions: Read the following case carefully. Answer the questions using the information in the case and in Chapter 8.

Julio woke up Tuesday morning with a scratchy throat and a runny nose.

"You really should stay home from school today to take care of your cold," his mother said.

"I can't stay home today. We have a test in Social Studies and the final soccer practice is today," said Julio. "The state regionals are tomorrow."

"Well then," said his mother, "you should eat a good breakfast and drink plenty of orange juice."

"I don't have time, Mom," said Julio. "I'm meeting Jim to go over our Social Studies notes before class." Julio left for school, picking up a doughnut to eat on the way. He met Jim on the steps of the school.

"Boy, I really feel lousy," said Julio, coughing. "I'm getting a cold, and I didn't get much sleep last night because Maria and I went to the movies."

"Why didn't you stay home today?" asked Jim.

"I didn't want to miss soccer practice," said Julio.

At soccer practice Julio missed passes and failed to take advantage of opportunities for two goals. The coach was upset and so were his teammates.

Julio went home after practice and went to bed. When he woke up the next morning he felt awful. His mother took his temperature. It was high. She called Dr. Roberts.

When the doctor came, she listened to Julio's chest. "I'm afraid you'll have to stay in bed for a few days, Julio. You have some fluid in your lungs," the doctor said. "I'll give you a prescription, but you probably won't be able to return to school before next Monday."

"Are you sure, Doctor?" Julio asked. "You know the regionals are today, and I'm on the soccer team."

"Sorry, Julio," said Dr. Roberts. "You don't want to end up in the hospital, do you?"

"No," said Julio. "But I sure am disappointed. The team was counting on me, too." He turned over and went to sleep.

1. What rules of good health and physical fitness did Julio break?

_____

_____

_____

_____

_____

2. How did Julio's illness affect his teammates?

_____

_____

_____

_____

_____

_____

3. How did Julio's illness affect Julio?

_____

_____

_____

_____

_____

_____

CHAPTER 9

CHOOSING
YOUR
LIFESTYLE

VOCABULARY PRACTICE

Directions: Complete the crossword puzzle using the Dynamic Terms learned in **Chapter 9.**

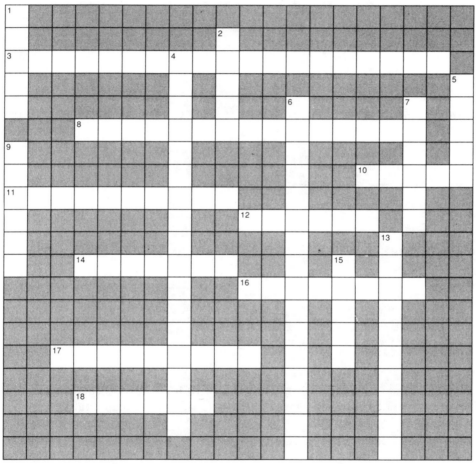

ACROSS

3. Physical items that provide comfort and pleasure and are desired as lifestyle traits.
8. Qualities that describe a person's lifestyle.
10. Items that are necessary for survival.
11. Gathering and studying information about your goals.
12. Phases of development that all people go through are called life ___ .
14. A person's financial worth.
16. Resources needed to buy lifestyle traits are called ___ resources.
17. The manner in which a person lives his or her life.
18. Ideas and beliefs that are important to you.

DOWN

1. Your knowledge, energy, and time are examples of ___ resources.
2. Earned income, interest, and dividends are called ___ .
4. Activities a person does when not working at a job.
5. The things a person desires but does not need to survive in life.
6. A measure of a person's necessities and comforts in life.
7. The things of value that a person owns.
9. To alter or make different.
13. Listing things in their order of importance for you.
15. Things you desire to achieve.

SHORT ANSWER QUESTIONS

Directions: Use your textbook, *The Dynamics of Work,* and your own personal experiences to answer each question in complete sentences.

1. What are two lifestyle decisions that you will make that will affect your standard of living?

_____

_____

_____

2. Explain how human resources are different from economic resources.

_____

_____

_____

3. List three assets that you currently own. How can the value of these assets be increased?

_____

_____

_____

4. List two lifestyle goals that are important for you to have now but that will probably change by the time you are 30 years old. Why will these lifestyle goals change?

_____

_____

_____

5. For most people, lifestyle goals related to leisure-time activities are very important. Explain why people place such a high value on their leisure-time activities.

_____

_____

_____

CHAPTER 9 • CHOOSING YOUR LIFESTYLE

DYNAMICS AT WORK—CASE 1

Directions: Read the following case carefully. Answer the questions using the information in the case and in Chapter 9.

As Nicole walked up the driveway looking at the house she has lived in with her parents, her brother, Todd, and her sister, Michele, since she was a baby, she thought about all the fun and the good times she and her family have had in the house. As she opened the door, she shouted "Hi Mom, I'm home."

"I'm in the family room," her mother answered. Nicole went into the family room and gave her mother a hug. "How was everything at school today? Would you like a snack before you begin your homework?" her mother asked.

"Yes, I would like a sandwich," Nicole responded. "School was really good. We talked about lifestyles today in our business class and the factors that determine and influence the quality of lifestyle you will have. We have to write a one-page report for homework that describes the type of lifestyle we would like to live as adults."

"Have you thought about the lifestyle you would like as an adult?" Nicole's mother asked.

"Yes, I was thinking about it as I came up the driveway just now. I want to continue the lifestyle I have now. I don't want it to change," Nicole responded.

"That is a really nice compliment for your dad and me. What is it that you like best about our lifestyle?" her mother asked.

"I like where we live. It is a nice house, and it is conveniently located to the park, the movie theater, and the shopping mall, and the city bus stop is at the corner. My friends also live in the neighborhood," Nicole answered.

"We learned in class today that the career you choose will be the most important influence on your lifestyle. I know that I want to be an accountant. With the salary that I can expect to earn, I will be able to afford a house like ours. I should also earn enough money to buy nice clothes and take a vacation each year. As an accountant, I will have the leisure time I need to continue playing tennis at the club."

"It sounds like you have your life all planned. Have you thought about your needs for having friends and perhaps a family of your own?" her mother asked.

"Of course! I would want to maintain the good friendships that I already have, and I am sure that I will meet other people at work who will have interests similar to mine and will become my friends. Even though Todd and Michele can be little pests at times, I would also want a family. I would like a husband like dad, and I think it would be nice to have two boys and a girl," Nicole said. "Well, I had better get started on this assignment. I'll see you at dinner time. Thanks for making the sandwich Mom."

"You are welcome, my dear," Nicole's mother responded.

1. Your most important needs and wants combine to form your lifestyle goals. When Nicole described to her mother the lifestyle she desired, which of her lifestyle goals were based on needs?

_____

_____

2. When Nicole described to her mother the lifestyle she desired, which of her lifestyle goals were based on wants?

_____

_____

_____

_____

_____

3. Which of Nicole's lifestyle goals relate to career satisfaction?

_____

_____

_____

_____

_____

4. Which of Nicole's lifestyle goals relate to family and/or friend relationships?

_____

_____

_____

_____

_____

CHAPTER 9 • CHOOSING YOUR LIFESTYLE

DYNAMICS AT WORK—CASE 2

Directions: Read the following case carefully. Answer the questions using the information in the case and in Chapter 9.

The Standkard family and the Zilinski family live next door to each other in an upper-middle class suburb of a major metropolitan city. Both families moved into the neighborhood five years ago, when the homes were first built in this housing development.

The Standkard family consists of a husband, a wife, a 10-year-old daughter, and a 12-year-old son. The husband and wife are both college graduates and work as professionals in the city. The family's yearly net income is $63,800.

The Zilinski family consists of a husband, wife, and two sons, ages 11 and 13. The husband is a college graduate and works as a dentist in the city. The wife is currently attending medical school at the local university. The family's yearly net income is $66,300.

The Standkards belong to the local golf and country club. They own two automobiles—a new BMW and a one-year-old Mercedes Benz convertible. The entire family dresses in current, designer-labeled fashion clothing. The Standkard family dines out about twice a week, sees all the current movies, and takes a two-week family vacation outside the United States each year.

The Zilinskis have a small swimming pool in their backyard. They own two automobiles—a new Ford Fiesta and a three-year-old Buick Regal. Mrs. Zilinski is a good seamstress and makes most of the clothing worn by the family. They frequently have barbecues in the backyard, occasionally see a movie in the city, and take a one-week fishing vacation at a nearby state campsite. Mr. Zilinski has an outstanding collection of rare stamps. Mrs. Zilinski is in her last year of medical school. She has been accepted into a residency program at the local hospital for next year.

The Standkard and Zilinski families have lived side by side for the past five years and are good friends. They enjoy each other's company, belong to the same church, and the boys play on the same little league baseball team.

1. Describe the lifestyle traits that are important for the Standkard family.

_____

_____

_____

_____

2. Describe the lifestyle traits that are important for the Zilinski family.

_____

_____

_____

_____

_____

3. What are the similarities between the lifestyle of the Standkard family and the lifestyle of the Zilinski family?

_____

_____

_____

_____

_____

4. What are the differences between the lifestyle of the Standkard family and the lifestyle of the Zilinski family?

_____

_____

_____

_____

_____

5. If you could choose to live either the lifestyle of the Standkard family or the lifestyle of the Zilinski family, which lifestyle would you choose? Explain why you selected this lifestyle. Based on your choice, list the lifestyle traits that are important for you.

_____

_____

_____

_____

_____

CHAPTER 9 • CHOOSING YOUR LIFESTYLE

PUT YOURSELF IN THE PICTURE

Directions: Describing your lifestyle provides valuable information, which you can use for self-assessment. It helps you focus on what is important for you in each major lifestyle trait classification—career satisfaction, family and friends, leisure activities, and material possessions. In the space below, create a lifestyle representation of either your current lifestyle or a desired future lifestyle. Your lifestyle can be represented by words, pictures, diagrams, collages, or a written essay.

CHAPTER 13

USING
FINANCIAL
SERVICES

VOCABULARY PRACTICE

Directions: Complete the crossword puzzle using the Dynamic Terms learned in Chapter 13.

ACROSS

2. An interest-bearing checking account.
4. A report showing transactions in a checking account for a one-month period.
9. An endorsement that limits the use of a check to a specific purpose.
11. The electronic process of handling financial transactions.
14. A check that has been paid by a bank.
15. A financial institution that handles transactions for its members.
16. The person to whom a check is made payable.
17. Lessened government controls of a business.

DOWN

1. An endorsement on the back of a check that makes it payable to anyone.
3. A check that is written for more funds than are available in the checking account.
5. A document that details deposits to a bank account.
6. Form attached to the check for recording details of the check written.
7. Fee charged by a bank for its services.
8. A special type of check sold by a bank for people going on vacation.
10. A bank that provides full-service banking.
12. A major source of loans for home mortgages.
13. The agency that insures funds kept in a savings account.
15. Paper money and coins.

SHORT ANSWER QUESTIONS

Directions: Use your textbook, *The Dynamics of Work,* and your own personal experiences to answer each question in complete sentences.

1. Compare the similarities and the differences among a commercial bank, a savings and loan association, and a credit union.

_____

_____

_____

2. Explain why a commercial bank is also called a full-service bank.

_____

_____

_____

3. What is the purpose of keeping either a check stub or a check register?

_____

_____

_____

4. What is the purpose of a signature card? A deposit slip? A withdrawal slip?

_____

_____

_____

5. Alex Doerr had a checkbook balance of $540 at the beginning of the month. During the month, he made deposits of $68.50 and $312.25 and wrote checks for $43.75, $113.70, $49.83, $16.75, and $110.17. What was the running balance in Alex's checking account at the end of the month?

_____

_____

_____

CHAPTER 13 • USING FINANCIAL SERVICES

CHECKING ACCOUNT TRANSACTIONS

Directions: Using the checking account forms provided on the following pages, prepare the deposit slip, fill out the check stubs, and write the checks as instructed for Kathleen Vinci's account. The beginning balance in Kathleen's account is $474.63

November 1	Write check 385 for $275 to Pablo Garcia for the November rent.
5	Write check 386 to Food Pic Supermarket for $23.86.
16	Write check 387 to Fairport Electric Company for $56.48.
17	Deposit: one $20 bill; 16 quarters; 70 pennies; a check for $28.50 drawn on the First National Bank, 65-148; and a check for $212.85 drawn on State Bank, 34-683.
30	Write check 388 to Tiffany Cohen for $20.

NO. _____ $ _____
DATE _____
TO _____
FOR _____

	DOLLARS	CENTS
BALANCE		
AMT. DEPOSITED		
TOTAL		
AMT. THIS CHECK		
BALANCE		

Kathleen Vinci   385
396 Culver Parkway
Rochester, MN 14548   _____ 19 ____   52-739
(516) 555-5359   1211

PAY TO THE
ORDER OF _____ $ _____

_____ DOLLARS

FIRST CITY BANK
Rush, MN 15623

MEMO _____   _____

⑆0711⑈1571⑆   385168⑈0365⑈

NO. _____ $ _____
DATE _____
TO _____
FOR _____

	DOLLARS	CENTS
BALANCE		
AMT. DEPOSITED		
TOTAL		
AMT. THIS CHECK		
BALANCE		

Kathleen Vinci   386
396 Culver Parkway
Rochester, MN 14548   _____ 19 ____   52-739
(516) 555-5359   1211

PAY TO THE
ORDER OF _____ $ _____

_____ DOLLARS

FIRST CITY BANK
Rush, MN 15623

MEMO _____   _____

⑆0711⑈1571⑆   386168⑈0365⑈

NO. _____ $ _____
DATE _____
TO _____
FOR _____

	DOLLARS	CENTS
BALANCE		
AMT. DEPOSITED		
TOTAL		
AMT. THIS CHECK		
BALANCE		

Kathleen Vinci
396 Culver Parkway
Rochester, MN 14548
(516) 555-5359

387

_____ 19 _____   52-739
1211

PAY TO THE
ORDER OF _____ $ _____

_____ DOLLARS

FIRST CITY BANK
Rush, MN 15623

MEMO _____   _____

⑆0711⑉1571⑆   387168⑉0365⑆

Kathleen Vinci
396 Culver Parkway
Rochester, MN 14548
(516) 555-5359

DEPOSIT SLIP

FIRST CITY BANK
Rush, MN 15623

52-739
1211

⑆0711⑉1571⑆   168⑉03265⑆

CASH	CURRENCY		
	COINS		
C H E C K S			
TOTAL FROM OTHER SIDE		
TOTAL		
LESS CASH RECIEVED		
NET DEPOSIT		

NO. _____ $ _____
DATE _____
TO _____
FOR _____

	DOLLARS	CENTS
BALANCE		
AMT. DEPOSITED		
TOTAL		
AMT. THIS CHECK		
BALANCE		

Kathleen Vinci
396 Culver Parkway
Rochester, MN 14548
(516) 555-5359

388

_____ 19 _____   52-739
1211

PAY TO THE
ORDER OF _____ $ _____

_____ DOLLARS

FIRST CITY BANK
Rush, MN 15623

MEMO _____   _____

⑆0711⑉1571⑆   388168⑉0365⑆

CHAPTER 13 • USING FINANCIAL SERVICES

WRITING ENDORSEMENTS

Directions: For each situation, write the endorsement as it should be written on the back of the check. In the space provided, identify the type of endorsement being used.

1. Suzanne Brennan endorsed a check in the simplest possible manner and transferred it to the Sutherland Boutique.

Type of Endorsement _____

2. Robert Strauss endorsed a check so that it was payable only to the Mendon Hardware Company.

Type of Endorsement _____

3. Tony Chen endorsed a check so that it would be deposited in his savings account SA126-37 at the State Bank of Arizona.

Type of Endorsement _____

4. Delia Pineiro endorsed a check so that it was payable to the order of Jon Curran.

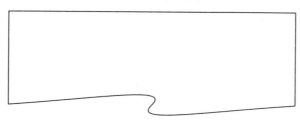

Type of Endorsement _____

RECONCILING A CHECKING ACCOUNT

Directions: In December, Kathleen Vinci received a bank statement dated November 28 that showed a balance of $98.94. Her checkbook running balance at the end of November was $365.24. In comparing her checkbook with the bank statement, Kathleen found that check 386 for $23.86 was outstanding; a deposit made on November 28 for $288.91 was not listed on the statement; and a service charge of $1.25 was deducted by the bank. Using the bank reconciliation form below, reconcile the checking account with the bank statement.

BANK RECONCILIATION STATEMENT
NOVEMBER 28, 19--

Checkbook Balance $_____   Bank Statement Balance $_____

Add: Add:
 Interest Earned   _____   Deposits in Transit
                                                      _____   _____

Total   _____   Total   _____

Deduct: Deduct:
 Bank Fee/   Outstanding Checks
 Service Charge   _____   _____ _____
                                                     _____ _____
                                                     _____ _____
                                                     _____ _____   _____

Adjusted Checkbook
 Balance $_____   Adjusted Bank Balance $_____

PAYING
TAXES FOR
GOVERNMENT
SERVICES

VOCABULARY PRACTICE

Directions: **Complete the crossword puzzle using the Dynamic Terms learned in Chapter 15.**

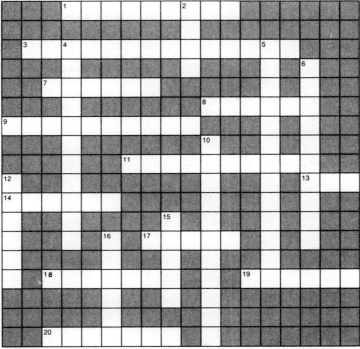

ACROSS

1. Type of business that uses income to further the purposes of the business.
3. Tax deducted from earnings, which provides income at the time of retirement.
7. Tax based on an individual's earnings.
8. Taxes paid on value of property left at time of death.
9. Personal expenses that can be subtracted from income before figuring taxes.
11. Withdrawal from work at the end of one's career.
13. A tax-deferred savings plan designed to save money for retirement.
14. Tax on the sale or use of specific products and services.
17. Tax imposed by state and local governments on products sold at retail.
18. Percentage of tax levied.
19. Value of goods, property, and money owned.
20. Statement of income earned and taxes deducted during prior year.

DOWN

2. Taxes deducted for Social Security payments.
4. Type of tax imposed on using a product or service.
5. Income taxed after exemptions and deductions are subtracted.
6. Amount of money earned but not taxed.
10. Taxes that take a higher percentage of income from high-income groups.
12. Formal statement of a person's income and taxes.
15. Required payments of money to the government.
16. Tax on products imported from foreign countries.

SHORT ANSWER QUESTIONS

Directions: Use your textbook, *The Dynamics of Work,* and your own personal experiences to answer each question in complete sentences.

1. What requirements must a taxpayer meet to file a 1040EZ Income Tax Return?

_____

_____

_____

2. What is the importance of the information contained in a W-2 Form received from an employer?

_____

_____

_____

3. Explain the expression "filing a tax return." What are the responsibilities of a taxpayer related to filing a tax return?

_____

_____

_____

4. Explain the similarities and the differences between an estate and inheritance tax and a gift tax.

_____

_____

_____

5. Identify one tax that is proportional, one tax that is progressive, and one tax that is regressive. For each tax, explain why it fits the classification selected.

_____

_____

_____

CHAPTER 15 • PAYING TAXES FOR GOVERNMENT SERVICES

COMPLETING A W-4 FORM

Directions: Read the following case carefully. Complete a correct W-4 Form (on the back of this page) for Katlin using the information in the case and in Chapter 15.

Katlin A. McCormick of 618 Parsells Avenue, Nampa, Idaho 83603 is a single, full-time high-school student who works part-time after school at her cousin's flower shop. Her Social Security number is 978-43-2010. Katlin paid no income tax last year, but she expects to earn between $2,000 and $2,500 this year. Her only other income is $75 in interest she earns from her savings account at the Community Savings Bank. Katlin can be claimed as a dependent on her mother's tax return.

19 Form W-4

**Department of the Treasury
Internal Revenue Service**

Purpose. Complete Form W-4 so that your employer can withhold the correct amount of Federal income tax from your pay.

Exemption From Withholding. Read line 6 of the certificate below to see if you can claim exempt status. If exempt, only complete the certificate; but do not complete lines 4 and 5. No Federal income tax will be withheld from your pay.

Basic Instructions. Employees who are not exempt should complete the Personal Allowances Worksheet. Additional worksheets are provided on page 2 for employees to adjust their withholding allowances based on itemized deductions, adjustments to income, or two-earner/two-job situations. Complete all worksheets that apply to your situation. The worksheets will help you figure the number of withholding allowances you are

entitled to claim. However, you may claim fewer allowances than this.

Head of Household. Generally, you may claim head of household filing status on your tax return only if you are unmarried and pay more than 50% of the costs of keeping up a home for yourself and your dependent(s) or other qualifying individuals.

Nonwage Income. If you have a large amount of nonwage income, such as interest or dividends, you should consider making estimated tax payments using Form 1040-ES. Otherwise, you may find that you owe additional tax at the end of the year.

Two-Earner/Two-Jobs. If you have a working spouse or more than one job, figure the total number of allowances you are entitled to claim on all jobs using worksheets from only one Form

W-4. This total should be divided among all jobs. Your withholding will usually be most accurate when all allowances are claimed on the W-4 filed for the highest paying job and zero allowances are claimed for the others.

Advance Earned Income Credit. If you are eligible for this credit, you can receive it added to your paycheck throughout the year. For details, obtain Form W-5 from your employer.

Check Your Withholding. After your W-4 takes effect, you can use **Publication 919**, Is My Withholding Correct for 1989?, to see how the dollar amount you are having withheld compares to your estimated total annual tax. Call 1-800-424-3676 (in Hawaii and Alaska, check your local telephone directory) to obtain this publication.

Personal Allowances Worksheet

A Enter "1" for **yourself** if no one else can claim you as a dependent . . . . **A** _____

B Enter "1" if:
{ 1. You are single and have only one job; or
2. You are married, have only one job, and your spouse does not work; or
3. Your wages from a second job or your spouse's wages (or the total of both) are $2,500 or less. } . . . . **B** _____

C Enter "1" for your **spouse.** But, you may choose to enter "0" if you are married and have either a working spouse or more than one job (this may help you avoid having too little tax withheld) . . . . **C** _____

D Enter number of **dependents** (other than your spouse or yourself) whom you will claim on your tax return . . . . . . **D** _____

E Enter "1" if you will file as a **head of household** on your tax return (see conditions under "Head of Household," above) . . **E** _____

F Enter "1" if you have at least $1,500 of **child or dependent care expenses** for which you plan to claim a credit . . . . **F** _____

G Add lines A through F and enter total here . . . . ▶ **G** _____

For accuracy, do all worksheets that apply.

- If you plan to **itemize or claim adjustments to income** and want to reduce your withholding, turn to the Deductions and Adjustments Worksheet on page 2.
- If you are **single** and have **more than one job** and your combined earnings from all jobs exceed $25,000 OR if you are **married** and have a **working spouse or more than one job,** and the combined earnings from all jobs exceed $40,000, then turn to the Two-Earner/Two-Job Worksheet on page 2 if you want to avoid having too little tax withheld.
- If **neither** of the above situations applies to you, **stop here** and enter the number from line G on line 4 of Form W-4 below.

- - - - - - - - - - - - - - **Cut here and give the certificate to your employer. Keep the top portion for your records.** - - - - - - - - - - - - - - -

Form **W-4** Department of the Treasury Internal Revenue Service	**Employee's Withholding Allowance Certificate** ▶ **For Privacy Act and Paperwork Reduction Act Notice, see reverse.**	OMB No. 1545-0010 **19**

1 Type or print your first name and middle initial | Last name | **2** Your social security number

Home address (number and street or rural route)

City or town, state, and ZIP code

3 Marital Status
- [ ] Single   [ ] Married
- [ ] Married, but withhold at higher Single rate.

Note: If married, but legally separated, or spouse is a nonresident alien, check the Single box.

4 Total number of allowances you are claiming (from line G above or from the Worksheets on back if they apply) . . . **4** ___

5 Additional amount, if any, you want deducted from each pay . . . . **5** $ ___

6 I claim exemption from withholding and I certify that I meet **ALL** of the following conditions for exemption:
- Last year I had a right to a refund of **ALL** Federal income tax withheld because I had **NO** tax liability; **AND**
- This year I expect a refund of **ALL** Federal income tax withheld because I expect to have **NO** tax liability; **AND**
- This year if my income exceeds $500 and includes nonwage income, another person cannot claim me as a dependent.

If you meet all of the above conditions, enter the year effective and "EXEMPT" here . . . ▶ **6** | 19

7 Are you a full-time student? (**Note:** Full-time students are not automatically exempt.) . . . . **7** [ ]Yes [ ]No

Under penalties of perjury, I certify that I am entitled to the number of withholding allowances claimed on this certificate or entitled to claim exempt status.

Employee's signature ▶ _____ Date ▶ _____ , 19 ___

8 Employer's name and address (**Employer:** Complete 8 and 10 **only if sending to IRS**) | **9** Office code (optional) | **10** Employer identification number

CHAPTER 15 • PAYING TAXES FOR GOVERNMENT SERVICES

COMPLETING A 1040EZ INCOME TAX RETURN

Directions: Read the following case carefully. Complete a correct 1040EZ Income Tax Return for Katlin using the information in the case and in Chapter 15.

On January 14 of the following year, Katlin received a W-2 Form from her employer listing the following information:

Katlin A. McCormick	Federal Income Tax Withheld:	$ 186.40
618 Parsells Avenue	Wages, Tips, Compensation:	$2,250.00
Nampa, Idaho 83603-1579	Social Security Tax Withheld:	$ 172.13
SS#978-43-2010	Social Security Wages:	$2,250.00
	State Income Tax:	$ 30.25
Sweet Flower Shop		
54 Westchester Avenue		
Nampa, Idaho 83603-1579		

Katlin also received a 1099-INT Form from her bank listing her interest income at $75. Katlin wants to contribute $1 of her tax to the Presidential Election Campaign Fund and can be claimed as a dependent on her mother's return.

Use the deduction worksheet and the tax table that follow to calculate the amount of tax owed by Katlin.

Line 4. If you checked the "Yes" box because you can be claimed as a dependent on another person's return (such as your parents'), complete the following worksheet to figure the amount to enter on line 4. For information on dependents, see page 12 of the instruction booklet.

Standard deduction worksheet for dependents

A. Enter the amount from line 1 on front. A. _____

B. Minimum amount. B. __500.00__

C. Compare the amounts on lines A and B above. Enter the LARGER of the two amounts here. C. _____

D. Maximum amount. D. __2,540.00__

E. Compare the amounts on lines C and D above. Enter the SMALLER of the two amounts here and on line 4 on front. E. _____

If 1040A, line 17, OR 1040EZ, line 7 is—		And you are—			
At least	But less than	Single (and 1040EZ filers)	Married filing jointly	Married filing separately	Head of a household
		Your tax is—			
$0	$5	$0	$0	$0	$0
5	15	1	1	1	1
15	25	2	2	2	2
25	50	4	4	4	4
50	75	7	7	7	7
75	100	10	10	10	10
100	125	12	12	12	12
125	150	15	15	15	15
150	175	18	18	18	18
175	200	21	21	21	21
200	225	23	23	23	23
225	250	26	26	26	26
250	275	29	29	29	29
275	300	32	32	32	32
300	325	34	34	34	34
325	350	37	37	37	37
350	375	40	40	40	40
375	400	43	43	43	43
400	425	45	45	45	45
425	450	48	48	48	48
450	475	51	51	51	51
475	500	54	54	54	54
500	525	56	56	56	56
525	550	59	59	59	59
550	575	62	62	62	62
575	600	65	65	65	65
600	625	67	67	67	67
625	650	70	70	70	70
650	675	73	73	73	73
675	700	76	76	76	76
700	725	78	78	78	78
725	750	81	81	81	81
750	775	84	84	84	84
775	800	87	87	87	87
800	825	89	89	89	89
825	850	92	92	92	92
850	875	95	95	95	95
875	900	98	98	98	98
900	925	100	100	100	100
925	950	103	103	103	103
950	975	106	106	106	106
975	1,000	109	109	109	109

Department of the Treasury - Internal Revenue Service

Form 1040EZ

Income Tax Return for Single filers with no dependents   **19**

OMB No. 1545-0675

Name & address

Use the IRS mailing label. If you don't have one, please print.

L
A
B
E
L

Print your name above (first, initial, last)

H
E
R
E

Present home address (number, street, and apt. no.). (If you have a P.O. box, see back.)

City, town, or post office, state, and ZIP code

Please print your numbers like this:

0 1 2 3 4 5 6 7 8 9

Your social security number

Please read the instructions on the back of this form. Also, see page 13 of the booklet for a helpful checklist.

Yes No

Presidential Election Campaign Fund
Do you want $1 to go to this fund?   *Note: Checking "Yes" will not change your tax or reduce your refund.* ▶

Dollars   **Cents**

Report your income

Attach Copy B of Form(s) W-2 here

*Note: You **must** check Yes or No.*

1 Total wages, salaries, and tips. This should be shown in Box 10 of your W-2 form(s). (Attach your W-2 form(s).)   **1**

2 Taxable interest income of $400 or less. If the total is more than $400, you cannot use Form 1040EZ.   **2**

3 Add line 1 and line 2. This is your **adjusted gross income.**   **3**

4 Can your parents or someone else claim you on their return?
☐ **Yes.** Do worksheet on back; enter amount from line E here.
☐ **No.** Enter 3,000 as your standard deduction.   **4**

5 Subtract line 4 from line 3. If line 4 is larger than line 3, enter 0.   **5**

6 If you checked the "Yes" box on line 4, enter **0.**
If you checked the "No" box on line 4, enter **1,950.**
This is your **personal exemption.**   **6**

7 Subtract line 6 from line 5. If line 6 is larger than line 5, enter 0. This is your **taxable income.**   **7**

Figure your tax

8 Enter your Federal income tax withheld from Box 9 of your W-2 form(s).   **8**

9 Use the **single** column in the tax table on pages 37–42 of the Form 1040A/1040EZ booklet to find the **tax** on the amount shown on **line 7** above. Enter the amount of tax.   **9**

Refund or amount you owe

Attach tax payment here

10 If line 8 is larger than line 9, subtract line 9 from line 8. Enter the **amount of your refund.**   **10**

11 If line 9 is larger than line 8, subtract line 8 from line 9. Enter the **amount you owe.** Attach check or money order for the full amount, payable to "Internal Revenue Service."   **11**

Sign your return

I have read this return. Under penalties of perjury, I declare that to the best of my knowledge and belief, the return is true, correct, and complete.

Your signature   Date

For IRS Use Only—Please do not write in boxes below.

COMPLETING A 1040A INCOME TAX RETURN

Directions: Read the following case carefully. Complete a correct 1040A Income Tax Return for Sergio using the information in the case and in Chapter 15.

On January 23, Sergio received a W-2 Form from his employer listing the following information:

Sergio R. Mendoza	Federal Income Tax Withheld:	$ 145.00
836 Vadillo Lane	Wages, Tips, Compensation:	$3,200.00
Portales, NM 75324-6175	Social Security Tax Withheld:	$ 244.80
SS#059-00-3212	Social Security Wages:	$3,200.00
	State Income Tax:	$ 73.40
Alamos Department Store		
264 Artesia Road		
Portales, NM 75324-6175		

Sergio also received a 1099-INT Form from the Garden National Bank listing his interest income at $900. Sergio wants to contribute $1 of his tax to the Presidential Election Campaign Fund and can be claimed as a dependent on his parents' return. Use the tax table that follows for calculating the amount of tax owed by Sergio.

Line 14d . If you checked the "Yes" box because you can be claimed as a dependent on another person's return (such as your parents'), complete the following worksheet to figure the amount to enter on line For information on dependents, see page 12 of the instruction booklet.

	A. Enter the amount from line 13	**A.**	
	B. Minimum amount.	**B.**	500.00
Standard deduction worksheet for dependents	**C.** Compare the amounts on lines A and B above. Enter the LARGER of the two amounts here.	**C.**	
	D. Maximum amount.	**D.**	2,540.00
	E. Compare the amounts on lines C and D above. Enter the SMALLER of the two amounts here and on line 14d	**E.**	

Line 16   Generally, you should enter 1,900 on line 6 as your personal exemption. However, if you can be claimed as a dependent on another person's return (such as your parents'), you cannot claim a personal exemption for yourself; enter 0 on line 6.

CHAPTER 15 • PAYING TAXES FOR GOVERNMENT SERVICES

If 1040A, line 17, OR 1040EZ, line 7 is—		And you are—			
At least	But less than	Single (and 1040EZ filers)	Married filing jointly	Married filing separately	Head of a household
		Your tax is—			
$0	$5	$0	$0	$0	$0
5	15	1	1	1	1
15	25	2	2	2	2
25	50	4	4	4	4
50	75	7	7	7	7
75	100	10	10	10	10
100	125	12	12	12	12
125	150	15	15	15	15
150	175	18	18	18	18
175	200	21	21	21	21
200	225	23	23	23	23
225	250	26	26	26	26
250	275	29	29	29	29
275	300	32	32	32	32
300	325	34	34	34	34
325	350	37	37	37	37
350	375	40	40	40	40
375	400	43	43	43	43
400	425	45	45	45	45
425	450	48	48	48	48
450	475	51	51	51	51
475	500	54	54	54	54
500	525	56	56	56	56
525	550	59	59	59	59
550	575	62	62	62	62
575	600	65	65	65	65
600	625	67	67	67	67
625	650	70	70	70	70
650	675	73	73	73	73
675	700	76	76	76	76
700	725	78	78	78	78
725	750	81	81	81	81
750	775	84	84	84	84
775	800	87	87	87	87
800	825	89	89	89	89
825	850	92	92	92	92
850	875	95	95	95	95
875	900	98	98	98	98
900	925	100	100	100	100
925	950	103	103	103	103
950	975	106	106	106	106
975	1,000	109	109	109	109
1,000					
1,000	1,025	111	111	111	111
1,025	1,050	114	114	114	114
1,050	1,075	117	117	117	117
1,075	1,100	120	120	120	120
1,100	1,125	122	122	122	122
1,125	1,150	125	125	125	125
1,150	1,175	128	128	128	128
1,175	1,200	131	131	131	131
1,200	1,225	133	133	133	133
1,225	1,250	136	136	136	136
1,250	1,275	139	139	139	139
1,275	1,300	142	142	142	142
1,300	1,325	144	144	144	144
1,325	1,350	147	147	147	147
1,350	1,375	150	150	150	150
1,375	1,400	153	153	153	153

If 1040A, line 17, OR 1040EZ, line 7 is—		And you are—			
At least	But less than	Single (and 1040EZ filers)	Married filing jointly	Married filing separately	Head of a household
		Your tax is—			
1,400	1,425	155	155	155	155
1,425	1,450	158	158	158	158
1,450	1,475	161	161	161	161
1,475	1,500	164	164	164	164
1,500	1,525	166	166	167	166
1,525	1,550	169	169	171	169
1,550	1,575	172	172	174	172
1,575	1,600	175	175	178	175
1,600	1,625	177	177	182	177
1,625	1,650	180	180	186	180
1,650	1,675	183	183	189	183
1,675	1,700	186	186	193	186
1,700	1,725	188	188	197	188
1,725	1,750	191	191	201	191
1,750	1,775	194	194	204	194
1,775	1,800	197	197	208	197
1,800	1,825	200	199	212	199
1,825	1,850	204	202	216	202
1,850	1,875	207	205	219	205
1,875	1,900	211	208	223	208
1,900	1,925	215	210	227	210
1,925	1,950	219	213	231	213
1,950	1,975	222	216	234	216
1,975	2,000	226	219	238	219
2,000					
2,000	2,025	230	221	242	221
2,025	2,050	234	224	246	224
2,050	2,075	237	227	249	227
2,075	2,100	241	230	253	230
2,100	2,125	245	232	257	232
2,125	2,150	249	235	261	235
2,150	2,175	252	238	264	238
2,175	2,200	256	241	268	241
2,200	2,225	260	243	272	243
2,225	2,250	264	246	276	246
2,250	2,275	267	249	279	249
2,275	2,300	271	252	283	252
2,300	2,325	275	254	287	254
2,325	2,350	279	257	291	257
2,350	2,375	282	260	294	260
2,375	2,400	286	263	298	263
2,400	2,425	290	265	302	265
2,425	2,450	294	268	306	268
2,450	2,475	297	271	309	271
2,475	2,500	301	274	313	274
2,500	2,525	305	276	317	277
2,525	2,550	309	279	321	281
2,550	2,575	312	282	324	284
2,575	2,600	316	285	328	288
2,600	2,625	320	287	332	292
2,625	2,650	324	290	336	296
2,650	2,675	327	293	339	299
2,675	2,700	331	296	343	303

Form

1040A

Department of the Treasury—Internal Revenue Service

U.S. Individual
Income Tax Return

OMB No. 1545-0085

Step 1
Label

Use IRS
label.
Otherwise,
please print
or type.

L A B E L   H E R E

Your first name and initial (if joint return, also give spouse's name and initial) | Last name

Your social security no.

Present home address (number, street, and apt. no.). (If you have a P.O. Box, see page 13 of the instructions.)

Spouse's social security no.

City, town or post office, state, and ZIP code

For **Privacy Act and
Paperwork Reduction
Act Notice**, see page 3.

Presidential Election Campaign Fund

Do you want $1 to go to this fund?. . . . . ☐ Yes ☐ No
If joint return, does your spouse want $1 to go to this fund? ☐ Yes ☐ No

Note: *Checking "Yes" will
not change your tax or
reduce your refund.*

Step 2
**Check your
filing status**
(Check only one)

1 ☐ Single (See if you can use Form 1040EZ.)
2 ☐ Married filing joint return (even if only one had income)
3 ☐ Married filing separate return. Enter spouse's social security number above
and spouse's full name here. _____
4 ☐ Head of household (with qualifying person). (See page 15.) If the qualifying person is your child
but not your dependent, enter this child's name here. _____
5 ☐ Qualifying widow(er) with dependent child (year spouse died ▶ 19 ____). (See page 16.)

Step 3
**Figure your
exemptions**

(See page 16 of
instructions.)

If more than 7
dependents,
see page 19.

Attach Copy B of
Form(s) W-2 here.

6a ☐ **Yourself** If someone (such as your parent) can claim you as a dependent on his or her tax
return, do not check box 6a. But be sure to check the box on line 15b on page 2.
6b ☐ **Spouse**

c Dependents: 1. Name (first, initial, and last name)	2. Check if under age 5	3. If age 5 or older, dependent's social security number	4. Relationship	5. No. of months lived in your home in 1988

No. of boxes
checked on
6a and 6b

No. of your
children on 6c
who:
● lived with
you
● didn't live
with you due
to divorce or
separation
(see page 19)

No. of **other**
dependents
listed on 6c

d If your child didn't live with you but is claimed as your dependent
under a pre-1985 agreement, check here . . . . ▶ ☐
e Total number of exemptions claimed.

Add numbers
entered on
lines above ☐

Step 4
**Figure your
total income**

Attach check or
money order here.

7 Wages, salaries, tips, etc. This should be shown in Box 10 of your W-2
form(s). (Attach Form(s) W-2.) | 7 |

8a Taxable interest income (see page 22). (If over $400, also complete
and attach Schedule 1, Part II.) | 8a |

b Tax-exempt interest income (see page 23).
(DO NOT include on line 8a.) | 8b |

9 Dividends. (If over $400, also complete and attach Schedule 1, Part III.) | 9 |

10 Unemployment compensation (insurance) from Form(s) 1099-G. | 10 |

11 Add lines 7, 8a, 9, and 10. Enter the total. This is your **total income.** ▶ 11 |

Step 5
**Figure your
adjusted
gross
income**

12a Your IRA deduction from applicable worksheet.
Rules for IRAs begin on page 24. | 12a |

b Spouse's IRA deduction from applicable worksheet.
Rules for IRAs begin on page 24. | 12b |

c Add lines 12a and 12b. Enter the total. These are your **total
adjustments.** | 12c |

13 Subtract line 12c from line 11. Enter the result. This is your **adjusted
gross income.** (If this line is less than $18,576 and a child lived with
you, see "Earned Income Credit" (line 23b) on page 34 of instructions.) ▶ 13 |

Form **1040A**

CHAPTER 15 • PAYING TAXES FOR GOVERNMENT SERVICES

19   Form 1040A
Page 2

Step 6	**14** Enter the amount from line 13.	14	

Figure your standard deduction,

15a Check if: ☐ **You** were 65 or older ☐ Blind ⎫ **Enter number of**
☐ **Spouse** was 65 or older ☐ Blind ⎬ **boxes checked** ▶ 15a ☐

b If someone (such as your parent) can claim you as a dependent,
check here . . . . ▶15b ☐

c If you are married filing separately and your spouse files Form
1040 and itemizes deductions, see page 28 and check here . . . ▶15c ☐

16 Standard deduction. See pages 28–29 for the amount to enter.	16
17 Subtract line 16 from line 14. Enter the result. (If line 16 is more than line 14, enter -0-.)	17

exemption amount, and

18 Multiply $1,950 by the total number of exemptions claimed on line 6e.	18

taxable income

19 Subtract line 18 from line 17. Enter the result. (If line 18 is more than line 17, enter -0-.) This is your **taxable income.** ▶	19

If You Want IRS To Figure Your Tax, See Page 29 of the Instructions.

Step 7

Caution: If you are under age 14 and have more than $1,000 of investment income, check here . . . . ▶ ☐
Also see page 30 to see if you have to use Form 8615 to figure your tax.

Figure your tax, credits, and payments (including advance EIC payments)

20 Find the tax on the amount on line 19. Check if from:
☐ Tax Table (pages 37–42) or ☐ Form 8615   20

21 Credit for child and dependent care expenses. Complete and
attach Schedule 1, Part I.   21

22 Subtract line 21 from line 20. Enter the result. (If line 21 is more than line 20, enter -0-.) This is your **total tax.** ▶ 22

23a Total Federal income tax withheld—from Box
9 of your W-2 form(s). (If any is from Form(s)
1099, check here ▶ ☐ .)   23a

b Earned income credit, from the worksheet on
page 35 of the instructions. Also see page 34.   23b

24 Add lines 23a and 23b. Enter the total. These are your **total payments.** ▶ 24

Step 8

Figure your refund or amount you owe

25 If line 24 is more than line 22, subtract line 22 from line 24. Enter the result.
This is the **amount of your refund.**   25

26 If line 22 is more than line 24, subtract line 24 from line 22. Enter the result.
This is the **amount you owe.** Attach check or money order for full amount
payable to "Internal Revenue Service." Write your social security number,
daytime phone number, and "1988 Form 1040A" on it.   26

Step 9

Sign your return

Under penalties of perjury, I declare that I have examined this return and accompanying schedules and statements, and to the best of my knowledge and belief, they are true, correct, and complete. Declaration of preparer (other than the taxpayer) is based on all information of which the preparer has any knowledge.

Your signature	Date	Your occupation
X		

Spouse's signature (if joint return, both must sign)	Date	Spouse's occupation
X		

Paid preparer's use only

Preparer's signature	Date	Preparer's social security no.
X		

Firm's name (or yours if self-employed)		Employer identification no.

Address and ZIP code	Check if self-employed ☐

19   **Schedule 1 (Form 1040A)**   OMB No. 1545-0085

Name(s) as shown on Form 1040A. (Do not complete if shown on other side.)   Your social security number

Part II   **Interest income** (see page 22 of the instructions)

Complete this part and attach Schedule 1 to Form 1040A if you received over $400 in taxable interest.
Even if you are not required to complete this part, you must report all interest on Form 1040A.

Note: *If you received a Form 1099-INT or Form 1099-OID from a brokerage firm, enter the firm's name and the total interest shown on that form.*

1 List name of payer   Amount

$
$
$
$
$
$
$
$
$
$
$
$
$
$
$
$
$
$
$

2 Add amounts on line 1. Enter the total here and on Form 1040A, line 8a.   2

Part III   **Dividend income** (see page 23 of the instructions)

Complete this part and attach Schedule 1 to Form 1040A if you received over $400 in dividends.
Even if you are not required to complete this part, you must report all taxable dividends on Form 1040A.

Note: *If you received a Form 1099-DIV from a brokerage firm, enter the firm's name and the total dividends shown on that form.*

1 List name of payer   Amount

$
$
$
$
$
$
$
$
$
$
$
$
$
$
$
$
$
$

2 Add amounts on line 1. Enter the total here and on Form 1040A, line 9.   2

CHAPTER 15 • PAYING TAXES FOR GOVERNMENT SERVICES

ALLOCATING TAX REVENUES

Directions: Read the following case carefully. Answer the questions using the information in the case and in Chapter 15.

Imagine that you are the mayor of Albion, Minnesota. Like all small towns, Albion receives financial grants from the federal government, which are used to help support its public services. For next year, however, in an effort to reduce the federal deficit, Congress has voted to cut the amount of federal aid it will give to local governments.

As mayor of Albion, you must recommend to the Town Board what to do about the reduced funding affecting six services. Presently these six services receive a total of $72,000 in federal support. Next year their support will be cut to $56,000. Each of these services must have at least as much in funds next year as they have this year, or they must be discontinued. If you recommend that a service be discontinued, you may reallocate those funds to another service. In making your recommendation, your choices are: (1) give the service the same amount of federal funds; (2) give the service more federal funds; (3) discontinue the service; or (4) give the service funds raised by a new local tax.

1. Indicate what you will be recommending to the Town Board by completing the following chart.

Service	Amount This Year	Amount Next Year	Source (Federal Funds or Local Tax)
Youth Recreation Center	$11,000	$ _____	_____
Drug and Alcohol Treatment Center	16,000	_____	_____
Senior Citizens Center	9,000	_____	_____
Crisis Pregnancy Center	10,000	_____	_____
Town Library	12,000	_____	_____
Emergency Shelter for the Homeless	14,000	_____	_____
TOTALS	$72,000	$ 56,000	

2. Who benefits the most from your recommendation? Why?

_____

_____

_____

_____

3. Who will be affected negatively by your recommendation? Why?

_____

_____

_____

_____

4. If you are recommending a new local tax, what type of tax will it be? Who will pay for the new tax—everyone or only some taxpayers? Why are you making this recommendation?

_____

_____

_____

_____

THE
MEANING
OF
CHANGE

VOCABULARY PRACTICE

Directions: Match the terms in Column *B* with the phrases in Column *A* by writing the letter of the term next to the phrase that best describes that term.

Column A

Column B

_____ 1. Unwilling to take a controlling interest in one's own existence.

_____ 2. A disagreement, usually involving a heated verbal exchange.

_____ 3. To become different or undergo transition.

_____ 4. A change over which an affected individual has no control.

_____ 5. One of a kind.

_____ 6. A disagreement serious enough to lead to combat.

_____ 7. A resolution of differences reached by mutual concessions.

_____ 8. A commitment made to do something or to deal with a situation, usually with a certain objective in mind.

_____ 9. A physical struggle or conflict.

_____ 10. A discussion or conference that resolves an issue.

A. external change
B. technological process
C. passive
D. decision
E. unique
F. conflict
G. combat
H. support
 I. compromise
 J. negotiation
K. argument
L. change

SHORT ANSWER QUESTIONS

Directions: Use your textbook, *The Dynamics of Work,* and your own personal experiences to answer each question in complete sentences.

1. Why is it true that although change requires decisions or actions there are no right or wrong ways to deal with change?

_____

_____

_____

2. What is the primary difference between a solution to a problem and a decision?

_____

_____

_____

3. Why should combat be avoided whenever possible?

_____

_____

_____

4. Why is uncertainty a form of internal conflict?

_____

_____

_____

5. What is the value of compromise in resolving a conflict?

_____

_____

_____

_____

CHAPTER 16 • THE MEANING OF CHANGE

SENTENCE COMPLETION

Directions: Using the list below, select the term that best completes each statement. No term is to be used more than once.

argument   passive
combat   problem
compromise   solution
decision   technological
internal change   uncertainty
negotiation   unique

1. _____ is something you want to cause.

2. Finding a _____ to a _____ often requires that you change your beliefs.

3. Rejecting a change is a form of _____ opposition.

4. As an individual, you have a _____ code of conduct.

5. _____ is a method of seeking a _____ to resolve a conflict.

6. One form of conflict that is always destructive is _____ .

7. _____ is a form of internal conflict.

8. A conflict among two or more people expressed in a verbal exchange is an _____ .

PUT YOURSELF IN THE PICTURE

Directions: Write a brief statement relating this chapter, "The Meaning of Change," to your everyday life. Describe a personal situation in which compromise helped settle a conflict. Explain how you achieved the compromise. How did the change affect you?

_____

_____

_____

_____

_____

_____

_____

_____

_____

_____

_____

_____

_____

CHAPTER 16 • THE MEANING OF CHANGE

DYNAMICS AT WORK—CASE 1

Directions: Read the following case carefully. Answer the questions using the information in the case and in Chapter 16.

Paul swung his bat in a graceful arc and sent the ball high and deep to center field, way over the fence. He grunted in satisfaction. When he had his timing down well in batting practice, he usually hit well in the game. The problem, he thought, was that he wouldn't have the right audience.

There was a modest crowd, of course. It was the team's first game of the season. The weather was just right. To the casual observer, everything seemed perfect.

But Paul had different feelings. A senior, he was beginning his third and final year on the varsity. Paul was an excellent all-around player. His coach expressed confidence that Paul would be offered a college scholarship, a professional contract, or both. Paul knew he could perform to those standards. As the first game was about to get underway, however, he worried that his play would go unnoticed.

Most professional scouts concentrated on winning teams, the league champions. Play-off games are showcases for talent like Paul's. The problem was that his team didn't have much hope of making the play-offs. The Jefferson twins, a highly talented pair, had been expected to carry the pitching load. However, two weeks before the beginning of the season, their father was transferred to another town by his company. The move meant a nice promotion for Mr. Jefferson. Unfortunately, it also cast a dark shadow over Valley High's baseball prospects.

Paul's coach walked the length of the dugout to where the powerful first baseman was sitting. "Are you ready for a fast start, Paul?" he asked.

"I sure am, coach, but I don't know what good it'll do if we can't make the play-offs," Paul said.

"Don't count us out yet, son. We'll miss the Jefferson boys, but I think we can still make a run for it. Anyway, don't let it get you down. Just keep doing your best. If you give up now, you'll be cheating yourself," the coach said.

"I'm not going to give up, coach. Losing the Jeffersons is rough, but I guess you're right. We still can be a pretty good team. And we sure have a challenge facing us now," Paul said.

1. What was the change described in the case?

_____

_____

_____

_____

_____

_____

2. Name four people affected by the change.

_____

_____

_____

_____

_____

3. For Paul, was the change an internal change or an external change? Explain why.

_____

_____

_____

_____

_____

_____

4. What was Paul's reaction to the change? Explain why you answered as you did.

_____

_____

_____

_____

_____

_____

CHAPTER 16 • THE MEANING OF CHANGE

DYNAMICS AT WORK—CASE 2

Directions: Read the following case carefully. Answer the questions using the information in the case and in Chapter 16.

Rita sighed in disgust as she dropped her books on the table. She sat down and looked across the table at her friend. "Did you hear the news, Jane?" Rita asked.

Jane saw the discouraged look on Rita's face. "What news, Rita? You look as though some great tragedy just struck."

"I just heard that Wendy is running for president of the student council. As far as I'm concerned, that would be a tragedy. I'll run against her if I have to. She would be a disaster as president," Rita declared.

"Why on earth do you feel that way? Wendy doesn't seem like such a bad person to me," Jane said.

"Well, she's bossy for one thing. And she's rather pushy, too, don't you agree?" Rita asked.

"I guess she can be that way sometimes," Jane agreed. "But she gets things done. Wendy may be just the person we need to head the council right now."

Rita thought a moment. "Well, I suppose she can have the job if she wants it. But I'm not going to let her boss me around. I'll just ignore her," she said.

"Then you're not going to challenge her in the election?" Jane asked.

"No, I think I can live with Wendy as student council president. I won't work for her, but I won't fight her either. I don't have the time," Rita said.

"That's probably the best course," Jane said. "Actually, I wouldn't be surprised if Wendy accomplished quite a bit as president. The principal really likes her, and having her mother on the board of education isn't going to hurt either."

"I forgot about that. Maybe she can persuade the school board to let us have that old lecture hall for a senior lounge," Rita said. The two girls stood, picked up their books, and headed for the cafeteria exit. "Maybe Wendy would be a good choice after all," Rita said. She smiled. "I think I'll vote for her, Jane."

CHAPTER 16 • THE MEANING OF CHANGE

Rita's reaction to the change that would come about with Wendy's election changed as her conversation with Jane progressed. Choose Rita's statement that best describes the following reactions to the change.

1. Opposition

_____

_____

_____

2. Rejection

_____

_____

_____

3. Acceptance

_____

_____

_____

4. Support

_____

_____

_____

CHAPTER 17

A PROCESS
FOR
DEALING
WITH
CHANGE

SENTENCE COMPLETION

Directions: Using the list below, select the term that best completes each statement. No term is to be used more than once.

alternatives   implement

commitment   model

consequences   symptom

evaluation process   troubleshooting

feedback

1. One type of _____ is a diagram of a process.

2. For a choice to be successful, you must make a _____ to support it.

3. _____ is a process used to locate and identify mechanical problems.

4. Dealing with a _____ usually will not eliminate a problem.

5. You _____ a choice when you commit yourself to carry out a plan of action.

6. You evaluate the _____ of _____ before you select a specific direction.

SHORT ANSWER QUESTIONS

Directions: Use your textbook, *The Dynamics of Work,* and your own personal experiences to answer each question in complete sentences.

1. Why is it important to evaluate the consequences of alternatives when solving a problem or making a decision?

_____

_____

_____

2. What is the relationship between a symptom and a problem?

_____

_____

_____

3. Why is it more difficult to evaluate consequences in decision making than in problem solving?

_____

_____

_____

4. What is the first question you should ask in a troubleshooting effort?

_____

_____

_____

5. What is the goal of the troubleshooting process?

_____

_____

_____

CHAPTER 17 • A PROCESS FOR DEALING WITH CHANGE

PUT YOURSELF IN THE PICTURE

Directions: Write a brief statement relating this chapter, "A Process for Dealing with Change," to your everyday life. Describe an important problem you solved or a major decision you made in the past year. Relate the method you used, and rate the success or failure of your actions. Would the outcome have been different if you had known and used the process method described in this chapter? If so, how?

_____

_____

_____

_____

_____

_____

_____

_____

_____

_____

_____

_____

_____

DYNAMICS AT WORK—CASE 1

Directions: Read the following cases carefully. Answer the questions using the information in the cases and in Chapter 17.

Julie opened the door to the auditorium just slightly. She peeked inside and saw the school choir rehearsing on stage. She listened for a minute and closed the door. "They sound really good today," she thought as she walked toward the library.

Singing in the choir was one of Julie's fondest ambitions. But she also wanted to run track in the spring. She would be unable to do both because choir rehearsal and track practice both take place every day after school.

Julie had a third factor to consider. She hoped to attend the state university to major in music. She would have to carry a heavy academic load for the next two years to qualify for admission. In addition, her grades would have to be excellent. She decided to speak with her counselor, Mr. Haven.

Julie knocked on the open door. "Come right in," Mr. Haven said. "Have a seat, Julie. What can I do for you today?"

"I'm trying to decide on an activity, Mr. Haven. I'm torn between the choir and the track team," Julie said. "Even more important, I'm not sure I can do either and keep my grades up. I don't want to do anything that might hurt my chances of getting into the state university."

"Let's see. You plan to major in music or music education, don't you, Julie? Let's take a look at the alternatives," Mr. Haven said.

Julie thought for a few moments. "If I keep improving in track, the coach said I have a good chance at getting an athletic scholarship. On the other hand, I really enjoy singing. And two of my best friends are in the choir. But what I'm really concerned about is whether I can keep my grades up while doing either of those things," she said.

Mr. Haven began writing. "It will help if we list the possible consequences of each choice," he said. "You may indeed win a track scholarship if you keep improving. On the other hand, you always run the risk of injury. Furthermore, the trend toward fewer scholarships will continue if the university faces further budget cutbacks.

"Two years in the choir would be a worthwhile experience for a music major, Julie. If you really enjoy singing, you might want to continue in college.

"Your grades are quite good. I don't believe that either activity would cause an academic problem for you. On the other hand, either activity could be enriching and rewarding.

"To summarize, Julie, if you base your decision on long-range goals, the choir seems best. If you base your decision on which activity you enjoy most, you can go either way," Mr. Haven said.

Julie stood up. "I think the long-range goal is my major concern, Mr. Haven. I can still run track with the local club next summer. Choir is something I know I can continue in college. I'm going to sign up for the auditions tomorrow. Thanks for your advice."

CHAPTER 17 • A PROCESS FOR DEALING WITH CHANGE

1. List the alternatives Julie had. For each alternative, list the consequences she had to consider.

<u>Alternatives</u>   <u>Consequences</u>

_____   _____

_____   _____

_____   _____

_____   _____

2. Was Julie solving a problem or making a decision? Explain why you answered as you did.

_____

_____

_____

3. Using a model as a guide, describe the process Julie went through.

_____

_____

_____

4. How did Julie's decision to join the choir relate to her code of conduct?

_____

_____

_____

DYNAMICS AT WORK—CASE 2

Charles called to his friend, Luis. "Hey, Luis, do you have a minute?"

"Sure, Charley," Luis answered. He excused himself from the group gathered in front of the lockers and walked over to the waiting Charles. "What's up?" Luis asked.

"Plenty, buddy," Charles replied. "I need some advice."

"No problem, Charley. Advice is always free," Luis joked.

"I know, Luis, but this is a real problem. I forgot all about that term paper that's due tomorrow in social studies," Charles said.

"You mean to say you haven't even started it yet?" Luis asked in surprise.

"That's exactly right. I just don't know what to do," Charles said.

"Why don't we analyze the situation," Luis offered. "The problem is that your term paper is due tomorrow and you can't possibly finish it in time. What are your alternatives?"

Charles looked up at the sky. "Well, I could run away from home . . ."

"Seriously, Charley. You could ask the teacher for an extension. You could make up some story about losing the paper. You could pretend to be sick and stay out of school for the final week before vacation. Do you have any more ideas?" Luis asked.

"Well, I'm not very good at making up stories. And, my folks would know I wasn't sick. I guess that leaves asking the teacher for an extension," Charles said.

"Honesty is probably the best policy, Charley. That's what I would do. You just have to commit yourself to spending the weekend writing that term paper—if the teacher is agreeable. You may have to skip the big dance, but that's better than having to repeat a class next year," Luis said.

"You're right, Luis. I'll survive missing the dance. I don't want to blow my chances of graduating on time. Guess I'll go see my teacher," Charles said.

1. Was Charles' "forgetting" about his term paper a problem, or was it a symptom? Explain your answer.

_____

_____

_____

2. In considering the alternatives that were suggested, how did Charles' code of conduct enter into his evaluation of those alternatives?

_____

_____

_____

_____
CHAPTER 18
_____

STRESS,
CONFLICT,
AND
PATHWAYS
TO PEACE

VOCABULARY PRACTICE

Directions: Match the terms in Column *B* with the phrases in Column *A* by writing the letter of the term next to the phrase that best describes that term.

Column A	*Column B*
_____ 1. A state that can occur in response to pressure or stress.	A. stress
	B. anger
_____ 2. A confrontation that involves large groups or communities of people.	C. tension
	D. group conflict
_____ 3. An underlying disagreement that remains unspoken and unresolved.	E. anxiety
	F. societal conflict
_____ 4. A disagreement or confrontation that involves two or more people on each side.	G. debate
	H. subdued conflict
_____ 5. Pressure or tension often caused by change.	
_____ 6. A discussion or argument that is guided by rules and procedures accepted by both sides.	

SHORT ANSWER QUESTIONS

Directions: Use your textbook, *The Dynamics of Work,* and your own personal experiences to answer each question in complete sentences.

1. When is stress unhealthful?

_____

_____

_____

_____

2. What is a subdued conflict?

_____

_____

_____

3. What advantage does an individual enjoy in group conflict?

_____

_____

_____

4. What is a major disadvantage of group conflict?

_____

_____

_____

5. What role does feedback play in the problem-solving/decision-making process?

_____

_____

_____

CHAPTER 18 • STRESS, CONFLICT, AND PATHWAYS TO PEACE

SENTENCE COMPLETION

Directions: Using the list below, select the term that best completes each statement. No term is to be used more than once.

subdued conflict	stress
debate	internal conflict
group conflict	societal conflict

1. War is an example of _____ .

2. _____ is a form of conflict that often brings positive results.

3. If you are annoyed by another person's actions, you have a(n) _____ .

4. Dealing with a conflict helps you to reduce _____ .

5. You always have others on your side in a(n) _____ .

6. Uncertainty over whether to carry your lunch to school or to buy lunch in the cafeteria is a

form of _____ .

PUT YOURSELF IN THE PICTURE

Directions: Write a brief statement relating this chapter, "Stress, Conflict, and Pathways to Peace," to your everyday life. Describe a group conflict in which you were involved during the past year. Were you a willing participant? Tell whether the conflict was resolved and, if so, how it was resolved.

_____

_____

_____

_____

_____

_____

_____

_____

_____

_____

_____

_____

_____

_____

CHAPTER 18 • STRESS, CONFLICT, AND PATHWAYS TO PEACE

DYNAMICS AT WORK—CASE 1

Directions: Read the following case carefully. Answer the questions using the information in the case and in Chapter 18.

Greg shook his head. "I don't know what I'm going to do, Alice," he said. "Just look at that bulldozer. It's ruining our practice field."

Alice looked up at her older brother. "It's really too bad, but you can't say it's a surprise. The sign announcing the new shopping center has been there for quite a while," she said.

Greg looked back as they passed the construction site. "I just wish there were something I could do," he said.

"Well, there isn't, Greg. I think you'd be better off if you'd stop worrying about the old practice field and start looking for a new one. You're getting all worked up over something you can't control," Alice said.

"I know, I know. But it just makes me so darn angry," Greg insisted.

"Listen, why don't you treat me to an ice cream cone, and we can talk about something else," Alice suggested.

"Okay, Alice. Will you finish typing my book report tonight for a double scoop?" Greg asked.

"That sounds fair," Alice said. "Will you stop complaining about your practice field?"

"Yeah, I guess so," he replied.

"Think of it this way, Greg. If you can't do anything about a situation, there's no use getting upset over it. You might as well move on to something else."

Greg laughed. "You mean like an ice cream cone?"

1. What was the cause of Greg's stress?

_____

_____

_____

_____

_____

_____

2. What method did Greg use to relieve his stress?

_____

_____

_____

_____

_____

3. What was Greg's real problem?

_____

_____

_____

_____

_____

4. What alternatives did Greg have that might help him solve his problem?

_____

_____

_____

_____

_____

CHAPTER 18 • STRESS, CONFLICT, AND PATHWAYS TO PEACE

DYNAMICS AT WORK—CASE 2

Directions: Read the following case carefully. Answer the questions using the information in the case and in Chapter 18.

Ben trotted slowly over to the bench. He was angry and frustrated. He had been wide open on that last play, but Dale threw the football in another direction. The result was an interception.

Ben sat near the end of the bench and tossed his helmet on the ground. He didn't know what to do about Dale. The quarterback hadn't thrown him a pass in three games. When one of the coaches mentioned this, Dale shrugged and said he hadn't seen Ben open on the play.

"I know I'm only a sophomore," Ben thought, "but I can catch the football as well as any senior. Dale just isn't giving me a fair chance."

Ben considered his options. He could confront Dale on the field or in the locker room and demand fair treatment. That approach might backfire, though, because Dale was the star of the team. Ben might gain a reputation as a complainer, and he didn't want that.

Another option was to approach Dale off the field and attempt to discuss the situation in a friendly manner. Ben had tried this earlier in the season, however, without success. Dale had said, "Listen, Ben, I'm running the offense on the field. My primary target is Gary. That's all there is to it." Ben knew that Gary and Dale were close friends. He also knew that Gary, a senior, was fighting to win a college scholarship.

The only other option Ben could think of was to involve a neutral third party. Another player could point out the problem to the coaching staff. The uninvolved player would have to be someone the coaches respected.

Ben looked down the bench. The person he needed was standing next to the head coach. Jim, the backup quarterback, was the perfect choice. He was being groomed to start next season, and he had a good relationship with the coach. Furthermore, Jim got along well with both Dale and Ben. He could be objective in evaluating the situation.

Ben decided to speak to Jim after the game. He knew he could present his case in an impersonal, factual way. Ben put his helmet back on. His team had the ball again. "Next week may be different," he thought as he trotted back onto the field.

1. What kind of conflict (internal, subdued, group, or societal) did Ben experience? Explain your answer.

_____

_____

_____

_____

2. Describe the process Ben used in trying to resolve the conflict.

_____

_____

_____

_____

_____

_____

3. What were the emotional factors involved in Ben's stressful situation?

_____

_____

_____

_____

_____

_____

**BUILDING
PROBLEM-SOLVING
AND
DECISION-MAKING
SKILLS**

VOCABULARY PRACTICE

Directions: Write a complete sentence defining each of the terms that follow.

1. reinforcement

_____

_____

_____

_____

_____

2. quota

_____

_____

_____

_____

_____

3. brainstorming

_____

_____

_____

_____

_____

SHORT ANSWER QUESTIONS

Directions: Use your textbook, *The Dynamics of Work,* and your own personal experiences to answer each question in complete sentences.

1. What is the major advantage of problem solving and decision making at the group level?

_____

_____

_____

2. What is the major disadvantage of problem solving and decision making at the group level?

_____

_____

_____

3. How does empathy contribute to the smooth functioning of a group?

_____

_____

_____

4. How is the brainstorming process organized and conducted?

_____

_____

_____

5. Why do some types of businesses use brainstorming as a continual process?

_____

_____

_____

SENTENCE COMPLETION

Directions: Using the list below, select the term that best completes each statement. No term is to be used more than once.

targets   reinforcement
brainstorming   quotas
estimates

1. _____ are often set at sales conferences.

2. Group problem solving and decision making has the advantage of _____ for ideas that are adopted.

3. _____ often involves writing down all ideas presented by members of a group.

PUT YOURSELF IN THE PICTURE

Directions: Write a brief statement relating this chapter, "Building Problem-Solving and Decision-Making Skills," to your everyday life. Think of a group problem-solving or decision-making effort in which you were involved. Examples might come from your family or from an organization to which you belong. Describe the process used. If brainstorming techniques were not used, consider whether that process would have made a difference in the outcome.

_____

_____

_____

_____

_____

_____

_____

_____

_____

_____

_____

_____

_____

_____

CHAPTER 19 • BUILDING PROBLEM-SOLVING AND DECISION-MAKING SKILLS

DYNAMICS AT WORK—CASE 1

Directions: Read each case carefully. Answer the questions using the information in the case and in Chapter 19.

Ruth called the committee to order. "I'm glad everyone could make this meeting," she said. "We have a big decision to make."

Ruth looked around the table at the other members of the student government finance committee. She knew all of them fairly well. She felt sure they would respond to the challenge.

"As you know," Ruth began, "Tommy Ford and his father were seriously injured in that car accident last month. Mr. Ford is covered by disability and other insurance, so the family can survive. But Tommy will need help to start college next fall. Since he won't be recovered from his injuries in time for football season, his scholarship will be limited to tuition and books. The student council has established a special fund to help Tommy through his freshman year. The council hopes to raise enough money to pay his room and board at the university. Our job is to plan an activity to raise the money."

Ruth looked at the other committee members. "We had better brainstorm this situation," she said. "Lester, as secretary of the committee, you keep track of all the ideas suggested. Who would like to offer the first suggestion?"

"How about selling candy or some other product door to door?" Ray asked. "Or maybe we could sell personal services like mowing lawns or doing yard work."

"Those ideas are worth investigating," Ruth responded. "The only problem is that we probably would have a lot of competition at this time of year."

"We could hold a series of car washes," Phyllis said. "They're fun, and people usually respond well."

"That's a good idea," Ruth said. "We shouldn't have any trouble finding a location. The only risk factor is the weather. We could get rained out."

"My uncle works at the daily newspaper. Maybe we could get the paper to sponsor a subscription drive," Lester said.

"That's also a good idea," Ruth said. "Don't forget to write down your own idea, Les," she laughed.

"Tommy was best known as a football and basketball star. Could we have a fund-raising basketball game? Maybe a faculty-alumni game or a varsity-alumni game?" Ray suggested.

"I don't know, Ray. There's a limited audience for that type of event, especially in the spring," Lester said.

"I know. Let's run a lottery on the campus," Chris said. "We'll make a million bucks!"

"Get serious, Chris," Ruth said. "You know that's illegal. Write it down anyway, Lester. Who knows what can happen? Now that we have some ideas, let's think about them for a day or two. Lester will make copies of the suggestions and distribute them to everyone on the committee. We can meet again Friday after sixth period. Is everyone available? If so, the meeting is adjourned."

As Ruth opened the Friday meeting, she noticed that Ray seemed eager to speak. "Did you come up with a winner, Ray?" Ruth asked.

"Could be," Ray answered. "Remember the lottery suggestion Chris made? Well, I thought about it that night, and I got the idea of a raffle. What if we sell tickets on a drawing for something valuable, like a car? People usually respond well to a raffle for something valuable."

"That sounds exciting," Ruth said. "But how would we go about acquiring a car?" she asked.

"Our next-door neighbor is a sales manager at the biggest dealership in town. I spoke to her last night, and she said she would check with her boss. She sounded encouraging," Ray reported.

"Good work, Ray," Ruth said. "As soon as you get an answer from your neighbor, we can meet again. And let's give Chris some recognition. Thanks to his lottery idea, we may have found our answer."

Explain how the steps in brainstorming were followed in this situation.

_____

_____

_____

_____

_____

_____

_____

_____

CHAPTER 19 • BUILDING PROBLEM-SOLVING AND DECISION-MAKING SKILLS

DYNAMICS AT WORK—CASE 2

Directions: Read each case carefully. Answer the questions using the information in the case and in Chapter 19.

Cynthia blushed and then apologized to the other cast members on stage. She had just missed a cue and had forgotten her next line. The other cast members tried to minimize the problem so Cynthia wouldn't feel too bad. But Mr. Butler, the drama club adviser, stopped the dress rehearsal. "We had better have a meeting," he said.

Paul, who had the lead role opposite Cynthia, put his arm around her shoulder. "Don't feel bad," Paul said. "That can happen to anyone."

Mr. Butler responded as the cast gathered around him. "I don't want anyone to feel badly. Cynthia, you are doing very well in this role. But this is the third time this week that you missed that cue, and the play opens tomorrow night. We don't want this to happen in front of an audience. So, let's consider our alternatives," he said. "Does anyone have any ideas?"

Jose spoke first. "Maybe we could change the cue—you know, make it more obvious."

"The trouble is that the cue would also be obvious to the audience," Maggie noted.

Paul had a different suggestion. "That line is not terribly important to the continuity of the play. I think I can make a minor alteration to my next line if it happens during the play," he said.

"That's not a bad idea, Paul, but it puts extra pressure on you," Mr. Butler said. "Are you sure you want to take that responsibility?"

"I'm sure I can handle it. But you're right. It would be somewhat risky," Paul replied.

Mr. Butler offered another idea. "Cynthia, if you feel uncomfortable at this point, it might be wise to let the understudy, Janice, take your place in the second act. With the costume changes, it wouldn't be that noticeable. I know you've worked hard to master the role, though, and I'd like to leave it up to you," he said.

"Maybe we won't have to do any of those things," Maggie interjected. "Cynthia knows the role very well. I think she can master that cue with some extra rehearsal tonight. Can't you, Cynthia?"

"Yes, I'm sure I can," Cynthia said. "I should apologize to everyone. I've been working extra hard to finish a term paper on time. I just haven't given the play enough attention during the past couple of weeks. If Paul and Jose can work with me tonight, I'm sure I can get through that scene all right."

"That would be the best solution," Mr. Butler said. "How do you fellows feel about it? Can you spend some extra time with Cynthia after rehearsal?"

"It's no problem for me," Paul said.

"Same here," Jose said.

"I can help, too," Maggie joined in. "I'm sure everything will be all right by curtain time," she said.

"All right, cast. Let's get back to our places on stage. We have a play to produce," Mr. Butler said.

1. What is the positive factor in group problem solving and decision making that is illustrated in this situation?

_____

_____

_____

_____

2. What part of the case illustrates the negative factor in group problem solving and decision making?

_____

_____

_____

_____

3. How did the group show support for Cynthia?

_____

_____

_____

_____

4. What alternatives were considered? From what source did each alternative come?

_____

_____

_____

_____

YOUR
RELATIONSHIPS—
THE NEED
TO BELONG

VOCABULARY PRACTICE

Directions: Complete the crossword puzzle using the Dynamic Terms learned in Chapter 20.

ACROSS

2. A promise to do something.
4. Almost no one is completely____-sufficient.
5. Interaction among two or more people.
6. Community of people who share common interests and needs.
7. Attention you recieve from other people and give back to them.
9. The core of all human social activities.
11. A club for students who are interested in buisiness.
15. Long-standing practices.
16. The way people form and conduct relationships.
17. Societal relationships that do not involve human emotions.

DOWN

1. A friend, fellow student, or co-worker who is your equal.
3. A group that operates within a formal structure and has specific goals.
4. Skills that a person develops that are learned from family.
8. Type of human-relations skills that help you get along with others in a positive manner.
10. An important person in relationships.
12. To recognize and understand the needs of another person.
13. People who share a common interest.
14. A relationship in which people take on specific roles.

MASLOW'S HIERARCHY OF NEEDS

Maslow's hierarchy of needs is based on the idea that all people have the same basic needs. An unfilled need will motivate an individual to act to satisfy that need. When a lower-level need has been satisfied, individuals then strive to fulfill their next level of unsatisfied needs. Maslow's hierarchy is a powerful tool for employers to use in motivating their employees.

Directions: For each level of needs listed below, list three ways in which an employer can motivate employees at that level.

Survival needs

_____

_____

Safety needs

_____

_____

Social needs

_____

_____

Esteem needs

_____

_____

Self-realization needs

_____

_____

Think about the motivators you have listed above. Which of these motivators would have the greatest power for motivating you to act? Your answer will be based on the unsatisfied needs you have today.

_____

_____

_____

CHAPTER 20 • YOUR RELATIONSHIPS— THE NEED TO BELONG

SHORT ANSWER QUESTIONS

Directions: Use your textbook, *The Dynamics of Work,* and your own personal experiences to answer each question in complete sentences.

1. Why is the subject of human relations important to all people?

_____

_____

_____

_____

2. What is the difference between relating effectively with another person and relating ineffectively with that individual?

_____

_____

_____

_____

3. Which is more important in the workplace: effective human-relations skills or technical job skills? Give arguments that support your position.

_____

_____

_____

_____

4. List five benefits an employee would receive from practicing effective human-relations skills at his or her place of employment.

_____

_____

_____

_____

5. Compare and contrast the similarities and differences between group relationships and organization relationships.

_____

_____

_____

_____

6. Being considerate is more than being polite. Write an example of a situation that illustrates consideration being given between two individuals.

_____

_____

_____

_____

CHAPTER 20 • YOUR RELATIONSHIPS— THE NEED TO BELONG

DYNAMICS AT WORK—CASE 1

Directions: Read the following case carefully. Answer the questions using the information in the case and in Chapter 20.

The loud crash almost caused Mrs. Nobles to drop the large pan she was placing on the stove. "What could that have been?" she wondered as she rushed from the kitchen. "What happened, Christine?" Mrs. Nobles called out as she reached the stairs.

"Oh, nothing, Mom. I tripped over Jerome's skateboard and fell. I threw it into his room, where it belongs," her daughter said.

"Did you hurt yourself, honey?" Mrs. Nobles asked as she started up the stairs.

"No, but I dropped my glass. My milk spilled on my dress, and now I have to change," Christine said angrily. She suddenly started crying. "Honestly, Mom, sometimes I wish Jerome had never been born."

Mrs. Nobles put her arm around her daughter's shoulder and hugged her. "Now Christine, you know you don't mean that. You love your little brother, even if he is a pest now and then. Don't you?"

"Yes, I do. But I wish he would be a little more considerate, Mom," Christine said, drying her eyes. She took another dress from her closet. "Now I'm going to be late for my VICA club meeting. Darn him."

"Fighting with Jerome doesn't help, dear. Maybe you and he should sit down and have a nice talk. Tell him how you feel. Ask him if he has any complaints about you. I'm sure there is room for compromise. If you both show a little more consideration for each other, you'll get along much better," Mrs. Nobles said. "Now hurry, or you'll be even later for that meeting."

"Okay, Mom, I'll try, but no promises. Why do little brothers have to be such pains, anyway?" Christine asked.

"I guess it's all part of growing up. You two will feel differently about each other in a few years. Your brother may well be one of the best friends you'll ever have."

1. For a personal relationship to be successful, six elements are required of the parties in the relationship. Which elements that are required for a personal relationship to be successful are missing between Christine and Jerome?

_____

_____

_____

_____

_____

_____

2. List ways in which Christine and her brother Jerome can show more consideration toward each other.

_____

_____

_____

_____

_____

_____

_____

_____

CHAPTER 20 • YOUR RELATIONSHIPS—THE NEED TO BELONG

DYNAMICS AT WORK—CASE 2

Directions: Read the following case carefully. Answer the questions using the information in the case and in Chapter 20.

Juan threw his towel into his locker. He looked at his best friend, Chien, standing in front of the next locker. "Well, Chien, there goes our last chance for a playoff invitation," Juan said.

"Yeah, thanks to good old 'Pistol Pete.' He just had to try for that last basket and be the hero of the game," Chien said. As they dressed, their teammate Pete, the top scorer in the basketball league, walked into the locker room.

"Hey, Pete, that was a nice shot at the buzzer," Juan said.

"Yeah, thanks for pulling the game out for us," Chien chided.

Pete walked to his locker. "Sorry, guys, but even I miss one now and then," he said. "You know how it is. When the chips are down, you have to go with your best shooter."

"That's true, unless one of your teammates is open, right under the basket," Juan said. "If you weren't so selfish, we'd probably be in the playoffs next week."

"Oh, was someone actually in the clear?" Pete asked.

Chien responded angrily: "Yes, Juan was open, and you would have seen him if you were a team player. Your trouble is that you only care about yourself, Pete. You may be the top scorer in the league, but we'll have a better team next year without you."

"Yeah," Juan agreed. "And playing basketball will be a lot more fun."

1. Which type of personal relationship is described in this situation?

_____

_____

_____

_____

2. Which elements that are required for a personal relationship to be successful are missing in this situation?

_____

_____

_____

_____

3. Were the statements made by Juan an example of using effective human-relations skills or ineffective human-relations skills? Why?

_____

_____

_____

_____

4. Were the statements made by Chien an example of using effective human-relations skills or ineffective human-relations skills? Why?

_____

_____

_____

_____

5. Were the statements made by Pete an example of using effective human-relations skills or ineffective human-relations skills? Why?

_____

_____

_____

_____

6. How could the script in this situation be written using effective human-relations skills?

_____

_____

_____

_____

CHAPTER 20 • YOUR RELATIONSHIPS— THE NEED TO BELONG

ASSESSING BEHAVIOR IN PERSONAL RELATIONSHIPS

Directions: Listed below are several different situations that you could easily encounter during a normal day. For each situation, identify which element necessary for a successful personal relationship is missing and then describe how effective human-relations skills could be used to improve each situation. Write your answers in the space provided.

1. In your business law class, Jim has misspelled the word "contract" in his answer to a case problem that he has written on the chalkboard. The students in the class are laughing.

Element missing:_____

The situation could be improved with effective human-relations skills by_____

_____

_____

_____

2. Phil has been named the employee of the week at work. You are angry and upset because you have been doing an excellent job and expected to receive the honor. When you see Phil, you say nothing to him about the award.

Element missing:_____

The situation could be improved with effective human-relations skills by_____

_____

_____

_____

3. Julia, a new student in your school, is being teased by some of your peers because she has a speech impediment. Although Julia looks hurt and angry, she says nothing in response to their taunts.

Element missing:_____

The situation could be improved with effective human-relations skills by_____

_____

_____

_____

4. Alicia worked hard on a display of review books in the bookstore showcase last week. She is upset because her marketing teacher, who is the bookstore adviser, has not commented on the display.

Element missing:_____

The situation could be improved with effective human-relations skills by_____

_____

_____

_____

_____

5. You meet your friend Fernando in the hall as you leave a conference with your social studies teacher. You are upset because you received a poor grade on your career project. Fernando keeps asking you what is wrong, even though you have told him you don't want to talk about it.

Element missing:_____

The situation could be improved with effective human-relations skills by_____

_____

_____

_____

_____

6. A friend who works with you in the student bookstore asks you to work the cash register for him this period so he can talk with his friend Stacey. This is the fifth time your friend has asked you to cover for him, but when you asked him last week to work for you so you could study for a test, he refused.

Element missing:_____

The situation could be improved with effective human-relations skills by_____

_____

_____

_____

CHAPTER 21

KNOWING
YOURSELF—
A GOOD
PERSON
TO KNOW

VOCABULARY PRACTICE

Directions: Match the terms in Column *B* with the phrases in Column *A* by writing the letter of the term next to the phrase that best describes that term.

Column A

_____ 1. Your priority of choices.

_____ 2. Using your hands to perform tasks.

_____ 3. Qualities that distinguish you as a unique person.

_____ 4. Your view of yourself.

_____ 5. Process for receiving and giving information about yourself.

_____ 6. Activities that you enjoy doing.

_____ 7. Your beliefs and feelings concerning work.

_____ 8. Your personal rules and beliefs that govern your behavior.

_____ 9. An unproven idea that you believe to be true.

_____ 10. Sensible concepts and ideas that are well thought out.

_____ 11. Total of your behavioral and emotional characteristics.

_____ 12. A person who prefers being alone.

_____ 13. Your basic outlook on life.

_____ 14. An outgoing person who prefers being with other people.

_____ 15. Using your mind to perform tasks.

_____ 16. Your beliefs and feelings concerning your existence.

_____ 17. Concepts that are not sensible.

_____ 18. Suggestions on how to conduct yourself in specific situations.

Column B

A. attitude

B. belief

C. code of living

D. extrovert

E. guidelines

F. illogical ideas

G. interests

H. introvert

I. Johari window

J. logical ideas

K. manual skills

L. mental skills

M. opinion

N. personality

O. preferences

P. philosophy of life

Q. philosophy of work

R. self

S. self-image

T. self-understanding

U. traits

PUT YOURSELF IN THE PICTURE

Directions: Write three paragraphs relating this chapter, "Knowing Yourself—A Good Person to Know," to your general sets of codes. In the first paragraph, describe your code about yourself. In the second paragraph, describe your code about other people. In the third paragraph, describe your code about the world.

_____

_____

_____

_____

_____

_____

_____

_____

_____

_____

_____

_____

_____

_____

_____

_____

_____

_____

CHAPTER 21 • KNOWING YOURSELF— A GOOD PERSON TO KNOW

SHORT ANSWER QUESTIONS

Directions: Use your textbook, *The Dynamics of Work,* and your own personal experiences to answer each question in complete sentences.

1. Compare the similarities and differences in the traits of a typical introvert and the traits of a typical extrovert.

_____

_____

_____

_____

_____

2. What parts of your self, other than physical traits, are constantly changing?

_____

_____

_____

_____

_____

3. What is meant by the hidden section of your Johari window?

_____

_____

_____

_____

_____

4. What is meant by the blind spot of your Johari window?

_____

_____

_____

_____

_____

5. What are the causes of change in your code of conduct?

_____

_____

_____

_____

6. Your code of living changes as you go through life. Compare your code of living today with your code of living two years ago. In a paragraph, identify which of the seven elements of your code have changed. Describe how these changes have affected your personal code of living.

_____

_____

_____

_____

_____

_____

_____

_____

CHAPTER 21 • KNOWING YOURSELF— A GOOD PERSON TO KNOW

DYNAMICS AT WORK

Directions: Read the following case carefully. Answer the questions using the information in the case and in Chapter 21.

Jeff grabbed his books and excused himself. "It was really nice meeting you," he said. "I have to run now, though, or I'll be late for practice."

Frieda and Ramona watched their new friend trotting toward the locker room.

"He sure is nice," Frieda said. "It's hard to imagine such a gentle person actually playing football."

"He really is a gentleman," Ramona agreed.

Frieda's brother, Collin, dashed up to the bench where the girls were sitting. "Will you take my book home, Frieda?" he asked. "I have to take some photos at practice, and I don't have time to go to my locker."

"Sure, Collin," his sister replied. "Say, how's that new player, Jeff, doing? Is he going to play Friday night?"

"You bet he is! Jeff is the main reason we're favored to win the league this year," Collin said. "It's going to be fun taking pictures of a winning team. We're just lucky his family moved into our school district."

Ramona agreed. "It looks like you became sports editor of the school paper at just the right time, Collin. But is Jeff really aggressive enough to be a football star? He seems so gentle and polite."

"Wait till you see him Friday night. He's a different person on the football field, a real tiger. He's one of the most aggressive players I've ever seen. It's hard to believe he's the same person," Collin said.

Frieda gazed toward the practice field. Speaking to no one in particular, she said, "I'm glad he's not that way off the field. . . ."

1. Describe the personality traits of the self that Jeff presented to Frieda and Ramona.

_____

_____

_____

_____

_____

2. Describe the personality traits of the self that Jeff presents on the football field.

_____

_____

_____

_____

_____

3. Why does Jeff display a different self to Frieda and Ramona than he displays on the football field?

_____

_____

_____

_____

_____

CHAPTER 21 • KNOWING YOURSELF— A GOOD PERSON TO KNOW

JOHARI WINDOW 1—WORDS THAT BEST DESCRIBE MYSELF

This activity will help you to increase your self-understanding by recognizing your weaknesses as well as your strengths. It requires honesty and objectivity if you are to learn to see yourself as you really are.

Directions: Read the words describing personality traits in Column *A* and Column *B* below. Decide which of these words best describes you. Circle the ten words in Column *A* and the ten words in Column *B* that best describe your perception of your self.

Column A	*Column B*
accepting	aloof
biased	candid
critical	clever
curious	close-mouthed
helpful	direct
inexperienced	frank
innocent	guarded
insensitive	noncommittal
joking	observant
judgmental	obstinate
keen	outspoken
modest	private
nosy	risk taking
persistent	shy
questioning	silent
receptive	sly
searching	straightforward
sincere	tactful
strong willed	unselfish
trusting	yielding

Total Points for Column *A* _____   Total Points for Column *B* _____

CHAPTER 21 • KNOWING YOURSELF— A GOOD PERSON TO KNOW

JOHARI WINDOW 2—WORDS THAT BEST DESCRIBE MY CLASSMATE

Directions: After you have completed the self-assessment part of the Johari window activity, give the next sheets to three other students in your class. Ask them to complete the activity, following the directions given in your self-assessment, to describe how they perceive you.

Column A	*Column B*
accepting	aloof
biased	candid
critical	clever
curious	close-mouthed
helpful	direct
inexperienced	frank
innocent	guarded
insensitive	noncommittal
joking	observant
judgmental	obstinate
keen	outspoken
modest	private
nosy	risk taking
persistent	shy
questioning	silent
receptive	sly
searching	straightforward
sincere	tactful
strong willed	unselfish
trusting	yielding

Total Points for Column *A* _____   Total Points for Column *B* _____

CHAPTER 21 • KNOWING YOURSELF— A GOOD PERSON TO KNOW

JOHARI WINDOW 3—WORDS THAT BEST DESCRIBE MY CLASSMATE

Directions: After you have completed the self-assessment part of the Johari window activity, give the next sheets to three other students in your class. Ask them to complete the activity, following the directions given in your self-assessment, to describe how they perceive you.

Column A	*Column B*
accepting	aloof
biased	candid
critical	clever
curious	close-mouthed
helpful	direct
inexperienced	frank
innocent	guarded
insensitive	noncommittal
joking	observant
judgmental	obstinate
keen	outspoken
modest	private
nosy	risk taking
persistent	shy
questioning	silent
receptive	sly
searching	straightforward
sincere	tactful
strong willed	unselfish
trusting	yielding

Total Points for Column *A* _____   Total Points for Column *B* _____

CHAPTER 21 • KNOWING YOURSELF— A GOOD PERSON TO KNOW

JOHARI WINDOW 4—WORDS THAT BEST DESCRIBE MY CLASSMATE

Directions: After you have completed the self-assessment part of the Johari window activity, give the next sheets to three other students in your class. Ask them to complete the activity, following the directions given in your self-assessment, to describe how they perceive you.

Column A	*Column B*
accepting	aloof
biased	candid
critical	clever
curious	close-mouthed
helpful	direct
inexperienced	frank
innocent	guarded
insensitive	noncommittal
joking	observant
judgmental	obstinate
keen	outspoken
modest	private
nosy	risk taking
persistent	shy
questioning	silent
receptive	sly
searching	straightforward
sincere	tactful
strong willed	unselfish
trusting	yielding

Total Points for Column A _____   Total Points for Column B _____

CHAPTER 21 • KNOWING YOURSELF— A GOOD PERSON TO KNOW

JOHARI WINDOW 5—AS I SEE MYSELF

Directions: Your teacher will read the words in each column that receive points. Add up the points in both columns on your self-assessment worksheet. Using the Johari window chart below, draw a picture of your Johari window.

Place an *X* on the top line of the chart for the points you received in Column *A* of your self-assessment. Place an *X* on the line on the left side of the chart for the points you received in Column *B* of your self-assessment.

Draw the picture of your Johari window from your self-assessment by drawing a straight line across the chart at the *X* and a straight line down the chart at the *X*.

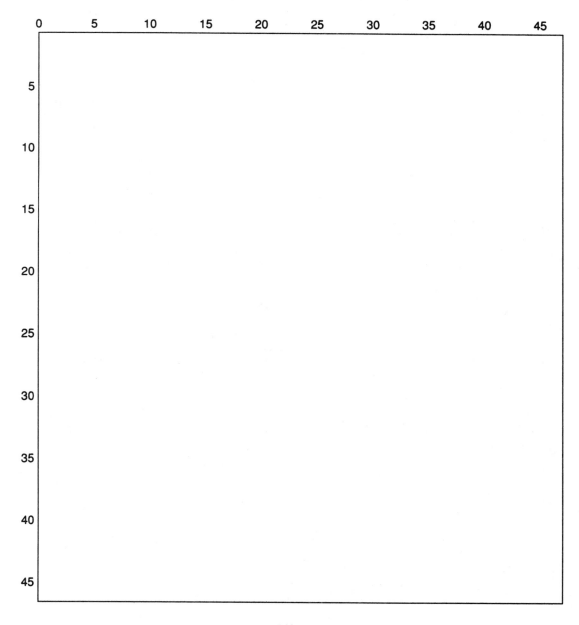

JOHARI WINDOW 6—HOW OTHERS SEE ME

Directions: Using the Johari window chart below, draw a picture of your Johari window as your classmates see you.

Total the points received on the three worksheets completed by your classmates for Column A. Divide this total by three. Place an *X* on the top line of the chart for the average score you received from your classmates in Column A.

Total the points received on the three worksheets completed by your classmates for Column B. Divide this total by three. Place an *X* on the left side of the chart for the average score you received from your classmates in Column B.

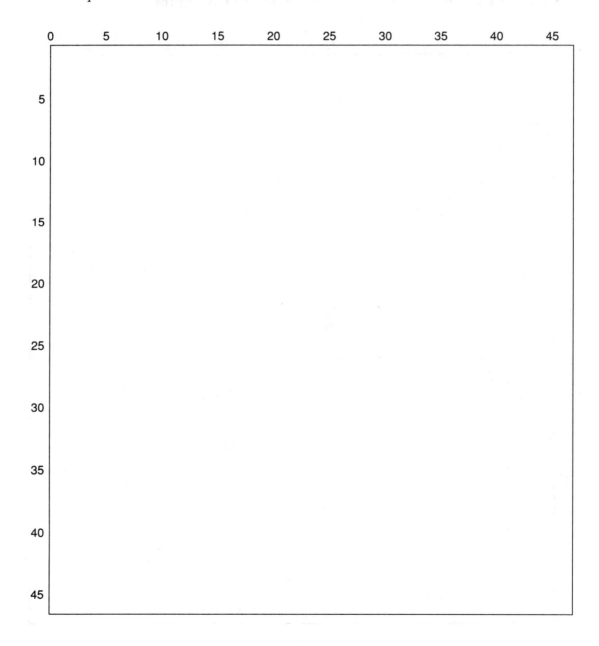

CHAPTER 21 • KNOWING YOURSELF— A GOOD PERSON TO KNOW

JOHARI WINDOW 7—DISCUSSION

Directions: Answer each of the following questions in complete sentences based on the information presented in the charts you have drawn of your Johari window.

1. Describe the similarities and the differences between the Johari window you completed for yourself and the Johari window completed by your classmates.

_____

_____

_____

_____

_____

2. List the areas of your Johari window that you would like to change. How can you either increase or decrease the size of these areas of your Johari window?

_____

_____

_____

_____

_____

3. Describe how the Johari window activity has increased your self-understanding.

_____

_____

_____

_____

_____

**PROJECTING
YOUR
IMAGE**

VOCABULARY PRACTICE

Directions: Complete each of the following sentences.

1. Having a self-confident attitude is important because

_____

_____

_____

2. Enthusiasm is contagious because

_____

_____

_____

3. Initiative is important on a job because

_____

_____

4. Aggressive behavior is inappropriate when

_____

_____

5. Having good posture means

_____

_____

6. I am optimistic when

_____

_____

7. I have confidence in my ability to

_____

_____

_____

8. A person with self-control can

_____

_____

_____

9. A person is loyal when

_____

_____

_____

10. Employers look for dependability in workers because

_____

_____

_____

Write a paragraph about your image that uses a minimum of ten Dynamic Terms you have learned in Chapter 22.

_____

_____

_____

_____

_____

_____

CHAPTER 22 • PROJECTING YOUR IMAGE

SHORT ANSWER QUESTIONS

Directions: Use your textbook, *The Dynamics of Work,* and your own personal experiences to answer each question in complete sentences.

1. Why is the image you project to others called a two-step presentation?

_____

_____

_____

2. Why do you see yourself differently from the way others see you?

_____

_____

_____

3. Which positive personality traits produce poise?

_____

_____

_____

4. Why is enthusiasm a desirable personality trait to possess?

_____

_____

_____

5. What are the major factors that will cause your image to change as you grow older?

_____

_____

_____

PERSONALITY INVENTORY

Directions: Objectively rate your own image by placing a check in the appropriate box next to each trait.

Trait	Excellent	Above Average	Average	Needs Improvement
Physical appearance				
Hygiene				
Grooming				
Dress				
Posture				
Self-confidence				
Motivation				
Enthusiasm				
Optimism				
Thoughtfulness				
Independence				
Initiative				
Organization				
Trustworthiness				
Loyalty				
Dependability				
Reliability				
Self-control				
Poise				
Bearing				
Self-assurance				
Tactfulness				
Outgoing nature				
Courteousness				
Friendliness				
Manners				
Respect for others				
Consideration for others				
Sensitivity				
Manual skills				
Manual dexterity				
Mental skills				
Self-understanding				

CHAPTER 22 • PROJECTING YOUR IMAGE

DYNAMICS AT WORK

Directions: Read the following case carefully. Answer the questions using the information in the case and in Chapter 22.

Juanita turned toward the kitchen when she heard the door swing open. "Hi Frances," she said. She was glad to have her friend join her behind the counter. The after-school crowd was starting to arrive, and they would be busy for the next couple of hours.

"Pretty busy, huh?" Frances observed. "Who's the guy with Mr. Sanchez?"

"Oh, he's the new cook trainee," Juanita replied.

Frances looked surprised. "What happened to Roberto? I thought he interviewed for that job."

"He did, but Mr. Sanchez turned him down and hired this other fellow," Juanita said. "I thought you knew."

"No, I didn't. I'm really surprised," Frances said. "Do you know why Mr. Sanchez decided against Roberto?"

Juanita leaned closer to Frances. "Confidentially, Mr. Sanchez was disappointed with the way Roberto looked," she said.

"What? Roberto is a great-looking guy, Juanita. I don't understand," Frances said.

"Roberto came over here right after football practice. He was tired and not dressed very well. His hair was messed up, and his fingernails were dirty. I guess Mr. Sanchez couldn't picture him working in the kitchen. Worst of all, Roberto was slouching. You know how Mr. Sanchez feels about posture. Roberto just didn't present himself very well that day," Juanita explained.

"That's too bad," Frances said. "Roberto is a really good worker and nice to be around. I hope he learned something from the experience."

1. Describe the first impression Mr. Sanchez formed about Roberto. Was this an accurate impression of Roberto?

_____

_____

_____

_____

_____

_____

2. Describe how Roberto should have dressed for the interview as a cook trainee with Mr. Sanchez.

_____

_____

_____

_____

_____

3. Which elements of hygiene and grooming did Roberto forget when he went for the interview with Mr. Sanchez?

_____

_____

_____

_____

_____

4. If you were Roberto's friend, what advice would you give him before he goes on another interview for a job?

_____

_____

_____

_____

_____

CHAPTER 23

GETTING
ALONG
IN THE
WORLD
OF WORK

VOCABULARY PRACTICE

Directions: From the following list, select the word that matches each definition, and write the word in the space provided. Locate the word in the puzzle, and circle the answers.

acquaintance	empathy	listening
assertive	feedback	optimist
authority	friend	respect
communication	leader	risk
delegate	leadership	supervisor

1. _____ A person for whom you have affection and respect.

2. _____ Mentally concentrating on what is being spoken.

3. _____ Having another employee perform a task for you.

4. _____ A two-way process for sharing information for understanding.

5. _____ A person whom you meet and deal with regularly.

6. _____ Presenting your ideas in a strong, confident manner.

7. _____ An individual who sees things positively.

8. _____ An individual who provides direction for a group.

9. _____ Gaining the cooperation of others to work together.

10. _____ Having the power or right to assign work to another employee.

11. _____ Being sensitive to the feelings of others.

12. _____ Taking a chance.

13. _____ A person in a position of leadership in the workplace.

14. _____ Return of updated, corrected, or evaluated information from the receiver to the sender.

15. _____ Admiring or appreciating the position of another person.

```
S  L  R  F  R  U  O  B  D  H  M  A  I  L  V  R  M  X  Z  Q  M  J
I  W  G  U  B  V  P  G  J  C  U  O  G  G  H  H  T  R  C  X  D  J
G  C  S  C  K  T  T  N  Q  J  I  V  C  Y  C  E  M  B  G  O  S  Y
S  W  U  X  M  U  I  Z  C  F  B  F  R  L  G  F  C  D  H  S  Q  G
Y  Z  E  I  G  T  M  M  U  E  W  E  N  Y  P  Q  J  U  H  E  N  T
M  N  R  T  G  G  I  Q  O  E  B  M  I  J  B  E  H  R  T  M  I  F
R  N  G  L  G  K  S  F  A  D  G  H  A  R  J  W  R  I  R  H  M  H
D  E  L  E  G  A  T  E  B  B  R  X  Y  C  V  I  Q  S  G  H  M  E
A  S  S  E  R  T  I  V  E  A  C  Q  C  Q  B  Q  T  X  O  H  O  Q
G  U  Y  J  A  C  R  K  A  C  C  K  G  T  E  N  I  B  V  C  X  R
U  V  T  F  N  D  F  O  W  K  O  Q  L  X  E  V  K  C  B  J  N  T
Y  Y  W  H  F  R  E  R  J  B  M  S  U  P  E  R  V  I  S  O  R  B
C  C  A  D  O  E  E  R  I  A  M  L  E  A  D  E  R  X  M  T  G  I
I  R  M  Y  P  R  J  S  S  E  U  L  M  L  I  S  T  E  N  I  N  G
F  G  U  O  P  L  I  I  P  H  N  W  I  Q  B  N  C  M  Y  F  X  Z
O  N  T  H  U  V  B  T  B  E  I  D  W  W  N  Y  T  P  I  F  Q  L
K  N  L  H  J  G  O  I  Y  I  C  P  N  Q  M  Z  J  A  V  B  D  W
S  D  U  E  I  P  F  W  J  V  A  T  O  T  B  F  K  T  N  Q  R  O
U  K  W  W  I  P  V  I  Y  V  T  Y  R  D  B  P  O  H  J  C  A  F
M  T  N  P  Q  G  H  S  I  R  I  S  K  O  M  D  K  Y  S  G  E  K
A  T  S  I  Q  U  Z  M  K  C  O  T  B  P  J  R  W  G  X  N  Y  L
H  C  V  J  I  T  L  V  C  C  N  H  H  B  O  S  L  L  B  N  U  H
```

CHAPTER 23 • GETTING ALONG IN THE WORLD OF WORK

SHORT ANSWER QUESTIONS

Directions: Use your textbook, *The Dynamics of Work,* and your own personal experiences to answer each question in complete sentences.

1. As an employee, what should you do if you start a job and then find that you do not understand the directions that were given to you by your supervisor?

_____

_____

_____

2. Explain the difference between hearing and listening. Give an example that illustrates hearing. Show how this example can be changed to illustrate listening.

_____

_____

_____

3. A supervisor is a model for his or her employees. Why is setting a good example an important aspect of good supervision?

_____

_____

_____

4. An empathetic person is able to judge another person's mood. Why is this important when you are trying to influence someone?

_____

_____

5. Do you think that you can ever become an effective leader? Give a minimum of three reasons that support your answer.

_____

_____

_____

CHAPTER 23 • GETTING ALONG IN THE WORLD OF WORK

DYNAMICS AT WORK—CASE 1

Directions: Read the following case carefully. Answer the questions using the information in the case and in Chapter 23.

Betty watched the moving van pull away from the curb and head toward the highway. She decided to go across the street and welcome the new family to the neighborhood. She had seen a girl who looked about her own age and a younger boy her brother's age. This could be interesting, she thought.

The front door was open when Betty walked up. She called through the screen door: "Hello! Welcome to Franklin Street."

Betty saw a figure coming toward the doorway. It was a teen-aged girl. "Hi! Are you a neighbor?" the girl asked, opening the screen door and extending her hand.

Betty took the other girl's hand. "I sure am," she said. "We live right across the street. My name's Betty."

"I'm Karen, and I'm glad to meet you. We're from out of state, and I feel kind of lost right now," the new girl said.

"Well, I'm sure you'll like it here," Betty said. "It's a nice community. Will you be going to my school?

"Yes. I'll be starting my senior year in September," Karen said. "It sure was hard to leave everything behind. I have no idea what to expect."

"Don't worry," Betty assured her. "We have a great bunch of kids, and I'm sure you'll fit right in. My family just moved here last year, and it's like we've lived here all our lives. You'll see. In fact, if you're settled in enough by tomorrow night, why don't you come with me to a party? You can meet most of my friends and get off to a good start."

Karen's face brightened. "That's great, Betty! I really appreciate your coming to my rescue like this."

"No problem. If we're going to be neighbors, we might as well be friends too," Betty said.

"There's one thing I'd like to ask right away," Karen said. "I'm hoping to get a summer job and a part-time job for the school year. Do you think I might find something?"

"If you like dealing with people, you might apply at the department store where I work. They're going to be hiring a couple more salespersons in a week or so. I can introduce you to my supervisor, if you're interested," Betty said.

"That's perfect!" Karen exclaimed. "I'm glad you're my neighbor, Betty, and I hope we can be friends."

"I'm sure we will be, Karen. I'll let you get back to unpacking now. If you need anything, just run across the street. You can meet my family—and I look forward to meeting yours—tomorrow," Betty said.

1. Are Betty and Karen acquaintances or friends? Give reasons to support your decision.

_____

_____

_____

2. Moving to a new community is the most demanding kind of change. What are some of the changes that Karen must make because of her move to this new environment?

_____

_____

_____

_____

3. How can Karen's relationship with Betty help her in adjusting to her new environment?

_____

_____

_____

_____

4. If you were Karen, what are three things you would do to help yourself adapt to your new environment?

_____

_____

_____

_____

CHAPTER 23 • GETTING ALONG IN THE WORLD OF WORK

DYNAMICS AT WORK—CASE 2

Directions: Read the following case carefully. Answer the questions using the information in the case and in Chapter 23.

Dan Sanfratello is the human-services manager for a small advertising agency with 60 employees. He has decided to have a party for the employees and has asked the other two staff members in his department—his assistant manager and his secretary—to come up with suggestions for the party. The only information about the party that Dan has told his staff is when the party will be held, how much money can be spent, and that the only purpose of the party is to build employee goodwill. He asked both of them to summarize this information before he ended his conversation with them to be sure that everyone had the correct information about the party.

After giving them a week to think of ideas for the party, Dan asked them for their suggestions at the weekly staff meeting in his office.

Mary Harvey, his assistant director, suggested having an open house at the agency for the employees and their families.

"That's a very good idea," Dan said. "It would give the employees a chance to meet socially and to show off the agency and their work areas to their families at the same time. If all 60 employees and their families came, we would not be able to comfortably fit all the people in our offices. If we decide to have an open house, however, we'll work out a way to accommodate all of the people."

Dan turned to his secretary and said, "Kathy, what do you recommend?"

"I thought that we should have an employee picnic," Kathy said.

"That's an excellent idea," Dan said. "It will take us out of the office, and the employees will probably enjoy the informality. I myself had thought of a dinner party, but I like your idea better."

Mary agreed that Kathy's was the best suggestion. Dan said that he would take care of the publicity himself. He then asked Kathy to arrange for the location and the food and Mary to take care of the entertainment and recreation.

Although Dan met with his subordinates, helped them with their assignments, and answered their questions, he let them make all of the decisions for the responsibilities that had been assigned to them.

The Saturday of the picnic came, and all went well—until the food was served. The food wasn't very good, but even worse, there wasn't enough for all of the people at the picnic.

The first thing on Monday morning, Dan's boss, Florence Seldin, was on the phone.

"The picnic was a fine idea," Florence said.

"Thank you," said Dan. "My staff thought of it."

"Unfortunately," Florence continued, "the food shortage just about ruined the picnic. Why wasn't enough food ordered for the picnic?"

"I miscalculated," Dan said. "I'll know better next time."

At the Monday morning meeting, Dan thanked Mary and Kathy for their help with the picnic. He also told them that he was thinking about starting an Employee-of-the-Month recognition program and asked them to come up with ideas for the recognition program by next week's meeting.

1. As a supervisor, did Dan give clear directions to the members of his staff and obtain feedback? Give specific examples from the case to support your decision.

_____

_____

_____

2. As a supervisor, did Dan delegate tasks to those under his authority? Give specific examples from the case to support your decision.

_____

_____

_____

3. As a supervisor, did Dan show consideration for the staff members under his supervision? Give specific examples from the case to support your decision.

_____

_____

_____

4. How did Dan contribute to Mary's and Kathy's self-esteem? Give specific examples from the case to support your decision.

_____

_____

_____

5. Evaluate Dan's leadership abilities as a supervisor. Give specific examples from the case to show that Dan was a good leader or specific examples to show that Dan was a poor leader.

_____

_____

_____

BUSINESS—
IDEAS
AT WORK

VOCABULARY PRACTICE

Directions: Match the terms in Column *B* with the phrases in Column *A* by writing the letter of the term next to the phrase that best describes that term.

Column A	*Column B*
_____ 1. A system in which economic questions are decided mostly by individuals in the marketplace.	A. profit
_____ 2. A need, or want, especially for goods or services.	B. supply
_____ 3. The quantity of a product or service that a firm is willing and able to make available for sale to meet demand.	C. capital investment
_____ 4. The value of an alternative that you might give up when you make a choice.	D. partnership
_____ 5. A gain made possible by a particular choice.	E. shares
_____ 6. The portion of revenue that exceeds expenditures.	F. goods
_____ 7. The total of all income received by an entity.	G. net worth
_____ 8. The resources, including money, needed to produce goods and/or services.	H. financial statement
_____ 9. The money invested in equipping a business.	I. market system
_____ 10. Physical items for sale; merchandise.	J. capital
_____ 11. An action that benefits others.	K. demand
_____ 12. A chance.	L. dissolution
_____ 13. A business owned by a single individual.	M. revenue
_____ 14. A business in which ownership and liability are shared by two or more persons.	N. liabilities
_____ 15. The process of breaking apart or dissolving.	O. service
_____ 16. An organized structure under which a business becomes a "fictitious person" with legal rights and responsibilities of an individual.	P. opportunity cost
_____ 17. The basic individual units of ownership of a corporation.	Q. assets
_____ 18. The governing body of a corporation.	R. accounting
_____ 19. A market in which securities (stocks and bonds) are bought and sold.	S. organization chart
	T. opportunity benefit

_____ 20. A diagram of the lines and levels of authority within an organization.

_____ 21. The process of recording, classifying, and summarizing business transactions and analyzing the information compiled.

_____ 22. A book of original entries listing, in order, all the transactions affecting a given area of business.

_____ 23. A report on the financial status of a person or business.

_____ 24. Property, money, and any other valuables owned by a person or an organization.

W. sole proprietorship
X. board of directors
Y. corporation
Z. stock exchange

CHAPTER 24 • BUSINESS— IDEAS AT WORK

SHORT ANSWER QUESTIONS

Directions: Use your textbook, *The Dynamics of Work,* and your own personal experiences to answer each question in complete sentences.

1. Explain what is meant by the statement, "Business is putting ideas to work."

_____

_____

_____

2. What is the relationship between return on investment and the profit of a business?

_____

_____

_____

3. Why is a corporation the most attractive form of business from the standpoint of risk?

_____

_____

_____

4. Why is a corporation looked upon as a "fictitious person"?

_____

_____

_____

5. What is the difference between inventory and plant?

_____

_____

_____

_____

SENTENCE COMPLETION

Directions: Using the list below, select the term that best completes each statement. No term is to be used more than once.

motivation	revenue
incentive	capital
soft good	hard good
stock exchange	patronage dividends
buying cooperative	organization chart

1. The equipment owned by a business is part of its _____ .

2. A person who has drive is said to have _____ or _____ .

3. _____ is money a business receives from selling its product or service.

4. Designer jeans are an example of a(n) _____ .

5. _____ may be earned by members of a(n) _____ .

6. Shares in corporations are bought and sold in a(n) _____ .

7. A(n) _____ illustrates how the functions of a corporation are divided.

8. A microwave oven is an example of a(n) _____ .

CHAPTER 24 • BUSINESS— IDEAS AT WORK

DYNAMICS AT WORK

Directions: Read the following case carefully. Answer the questions using the information in the case and in Chapter 24.

Danny swung his shoeshine box from his shoulder and placed it on the sidewalk. He positioned the box near the corner of the building. He looked at his younger brother, who was waiting for instructions.

"Always put your stand at a corner, Joey. That way you catch the people walking in two directions. In the middle of the block, you'll miss the guys crossing the street," Danny advised.

Joey nodded. "I see what you mean," he said. "Is this your corner, Danny?"

"It is as long as I get here first," Danny replied. "That older guy, Pat, who lives over near the park sometimes beats me to it. We have an agreement. First one here gets the corner. The other guy finds another spot. That's why I leave so early in the morning. This is the best spot in town."

"Where do you want me to set up?" Joey asked.

"You just stay with me this morning. I'll let you meet some of my customers, so you can get an idea of how this works. Tomorrow, I'll show you another good spot. If Pat tries to move you out, we'll have to work out a new agreement," Danny said.

Joey laughed. "Yeah, and I'll bet everyone better stand clear while you're negotiating, huh?"

"Well, Joey, that's one of the risks in this business. You have to learn to deal with your competition," Danny said.

1. What were Danny's capital goods?

_____

_____

_____

2. Did Danny have a "place of business"? What was it?

_____

_____

_____

3. What were the risks that Danny took?

_____

_____

_____

PUTTING YOURSELF IN THE PICTURE

Directions: Write a brief statement relating this chapter, "Business—Ideas at Work," to your everyday life. Of the businesses with which you or your family deal regularly, which do you think has the greatest capital investment? Describe the kinds of capital goods involved in that business.

_____

_____

_____

_____

_____

_____

_____

_____

_____

_____

_____

_____

_____

_____

_____

_____

_____

BUSINESS
AND
ECONOMICS

VOCABULARY PRACTICE

Directions: Match the terms in Column *B* with the phrases in Column *A* by writing the letter of the term next to the phrase that best describes that term.

Column A

_____ 1. An economic system in which the government owns and controls economic resources.

_____ 2. The point at which the demand curve and the supply curve intersect.

_____ 3. When supply exceeds demand.

_____ 4. The study of demand, supply, and the allocation of resources.

_____ 5. A stoppage of commerce.

_____ 6. Requirements supplied by nature.

_____ 7. A market situation in which a business operates without competition.

_____ 8. An economy using the principle of both free enterprise and a controlled economy.

Column B

A. economics
B. natural resources
C. utility
D. command economy
E. mixed economy
F. market price
G. surplus
H. embargo
I. shortage
J. monopoly

SHORT ANSWER QUESTIONS

Directions: Use your textbook, *The Dynamics of Work,* and your own personal experiences to answer each question in complete sentences.

1. In economic terms, what is meant by a shortage?

_____

_____

_____

2. What is the basic difference between a command economy and a free market economy?

_____

_____

_____

3. How does the role of the consumer differ in command and free market economies?

_____

_____

_____

4. What is the major advantage of competition to consumers in a free market?

_____

_____

_____

5. What is a monopoly?

_____

_____

_____

CHAPTER 25 • BUSINESS AND ECONOMICS

SENTENCE COMPLETION·

Directions: Using the list below, select the term that best completes each statement. No term is to be used more than once.

socialism	surplus
communism	shortage
controlled economy	competition
combined economic system	utility
law of demand	monopoly

1. A _____ has some of the elements of both a free market and a

   _____ .

2. _____ is a system in which individuals have little control over their careers.

3. The _____ says that consumers usually buy more at lower prices and less at higher prices.

4. A business operating a _____ has no _____ from other businesses.

5. _____ is a system in which government owns and operates all or most of the means of production and distribution.

6. When consumers want more of a product than is available, a _____ occurs.

7. Competition enables consumers to compare the quality, appearance, and _____

   _____ of products as well as their prices.

8. If a _____ of a consumer good exists, its price will tend to be driven lower.

DYNAMICS AT WORK

Directions: Read the following case carefully. Answer the questions using the information below and in Chapter 25.

Bill lifted the front of his bike to place the wheel in the rack. He wrapped the chain around the frame and locked it securely. Al and Julio were leaning against the fence of the community center swimming pool. Bill walked over to greet them.

"How's the water, guys?" he asked.

"Hey, Bill. Where have you been? We were getting worried about you, man," Al said.

"Yeah," Julio agreed. "We thought you were going to be here early. Did you oversleep or what?"

"No," Bill said. "I was out looking for a summer job. Man, it is rough out there. It seems like nobody's hiring, period."

"That's the picture, all right," Julio said. "My dad says it's the economy."

"I thought the economy was getting better," Al said. "The television newspeople keep saying that we're in the middle of a recovery."

"I'm talking about the local economy, man," Julio explained. "There's a lot of people out of work. Ever since they closed that car assembly plant over in Jonesville, things have been bad around here. In fact, all the towns around here are hurting. More than a thousand people were laid off when the plant closed."

"That's bad news," Bill said. "It looks as if there won't be any summer jobs this year."

"Don't give up hope, yet. My mother heard rumors that the assembly plant may be reopened next month. She said car sales are up because the national economy is doing better. The word is that the plant will be needed again," Al said.

"Well, that sure would help the local economy," Julio said. "It's rough when so many people work at the same factory, and it gets closed down."

1. Why would the local economy in Bill's town be different from the national economy?

_____

_____

_____

_____

2. What effect will the national economy have on Bill's summer job?

_____

_____

_____

_____

THE
ECONOMIC
SYSTEM

VOCABULARY PRACTICE

Directions: Match the terms in Column *B* with the phrases in Column *A* by writing the letter of the term next to the phrases that best describes that term.

Column A	*Column B*
_____ 1. A right or license to operate a business in a certain territory.	A. franchise
_____ 2. A prescribed, or unchanging, rate of income.	B. trust
_____ 3. An agreement between businesses aimed at reducing competition.	C. zoning ordinance
_____ 4. A market in which securities are bought and sold.	D. inflation
_____ 5. A product or item purchased to equip a business.	E. fixed income
_____ 6. A market situation in which a business operates without competition.	F. stock exchange
_____ 7. Establishes rules for land usage and building construction.	G. commodity
_____ 8. To watch or keep track of.	H. capital good
_____ 9. An agricultural or mining product that can be stored in large quantities.	I. monitor
_____ 10. An increase in prices leading to a decline in purchasing power.	J. monopoly

SHORT ANSWER QUESTIONS

Directions: Use your textbook, *The Dynamics of Work,* and your own personal experiences to answer each question in complete sentences.

1. Why do certain resources belong to the people?

_____

_____

_____

_____

2. What are the special public concerns that apply in the area of nuclear energy?

_____

_____

_____

_____

3. Why is a monopoly harmful to the public?

_____

_____

_____

4. What is the purpose of a usury law?

_____

_____

_____

_____

5. What is indicated by an increase in capital goods orders?

_____

_____

_____

CHAPTER 26 • THE ECONOMIC SYSTEM

SENTENCE COMPLETION

Directions: Using the list below, select the term that best completes each statement. No term is to be used more than once.

monitor	quasi-public
zoning ordinances	building codes
inflation	fixed income
stock exchange	economic indicator
capital good	per capita income

1. If their incomes are equal, a childless couple has a higher _____ than a couple with three children.

2. A high _____ rate is hardest on retired persons and others who live on a

   _____ .

3. The laws that have the greatest impact on a contractor are a city's _____ and

   _____ .

4. Some utility companies are _____ agencies.

5. Government, private businesses, and individuals _____ the economy to make informed decisions.

6. Listed securities are sold at a _____ .

7. The gross national product (GNP) is a leading _____ .

8. An example of a _____ is a computer.

PUT YOURSELF IN THE PICTURE

Directions: Write a brief statement relating this chapter, "The Economic System," to your everyday life. Identify any licensed individuals with whom you or your family deal on a regular basis. State the sources of authority for the various licenses (state, county, city). Which of these individuals do you think had to study longest in preparation for licensing examinations?

_____

_____

_____

_____

_____

_____

_____

_____

_____

_____

_____

_____

_____

_____

_____

_____

_____

_____

THE ROLE
OF BUSINESS
AND
GOVERNMENT

VOCABULARY PRACTICE

Directions: Match the terms in Column *B* with the phrases in Column *A* by writing the letter of the term next to the phrase that best describes that term.

Column A

_____ 1. Products or items.

_____ 2. Tasks that people or machines perform for us.

_____ 3. Actual thing, capable of being touched.

_____ 4. Incapable of being perceived by the sense of touch.

_____ 5. Any knowledge gained through communication, research, or instruction.

_____ 6. To create something having exchange value.

_____ 7. Land, labor, capital, and management, which are the resources needed to produce products, services, and information.

_____ 8. The ability to put together a business to make goods or provide services.

_____ 9. Materials supplied by nature and then used by people.

_____ 10 The ability of goods or services to satisfy human wants.

_____ 11. The act of using goods and services to satisfy our wants and needs.

_____ 12. Controlling operations of a process, system, or apparatus by mechanical or electrical devices.

_____ 13. The use of any resource or resources to the best advantage.

_____ 14. The amount of output resulting from the use of a resource.

_____ 15. An organization in which excess income is used to further the purposes for which the organization was founded.

_____ 16. A construction project intended for public ownership and use.

_____ 17. A tax levied on minerals extracted from publicly owned land.

_____ 18. A situation resulting from the attitude of a community toward business.

_____ 19 A description of the recirculation of money spent by a business through an area's economy.

_____ 20. A tax levied on specific retail products.

Column B

A. automation

B. entrepreneurship

C. tangible

D. nonprofit business

E. multiplier effect

F. public works project

G. goods

H. information

I. utility

J. severance tax

K. intangible

L. services

M. consumption

N. productivity

O. produce

P. business climate

Q. factors of production

R. material

S. specialization

T. selective sales tax

U. natural resources

SHORT ANSWER QUESTIONS

Directions: Use your textbook, *The Dynamics of Work,* and your own personal experiences to answer each question in complete sentences.

1. How do consumers benefit from the American production system?

_____

_____

_____

2. What are some examples of producers of services rather than goods?

_____

_____

_____

3. Why is the operation of government similar to that of a nonprofit business?

_____

_____

_____

4. What are the three areas in which government ranks as a major producer?

_____

_____

_____

5. How does government serve the public by regulating certain businesses and industries?

_____

_____

_____

CHAPTER 27 • THE ROLE OF BUSINESS AND GOVERNMENT

SENTENCE COMPLETION

Directions: Using the list below, select the term that best completes each statement. No term is to be used more than once.

community   business climate
nonprofit business   grant
tangible   severance tax
public works project   intangible
factors of production

1. New businesses are likely to be attracted to a _____ with a good

   _____ .

2. A government _____ is a typical means of funding a research project.

3. A product is usually _____ , while a service is usually _____ .

4. Entrepreneurship is one of the most important _____ .

5. Government in the role of producer can be likened to a _____ .

6. Miners using public lands may be asked to pay a _____ on the ore they extract from their mines.

7. A bridge or a dam constructed in your community is an example of a _____ .

DYNAMICS AT WORK

Directions: Read the following case carefully. Answer the questions using the information below and in Chapter 27.

The flashing lights of the emergency vehicles reflected off the windows of the houses across the street. A light rain was falling, and Ted felt the early evening scene could have come from a television show.

But it was real. The paramedics were placing the man into the ambulance to be transported to the hospital. Ted couldn't see much from the living room window.

"Do you think Mr. Patterson will be all right, Mom?" Ted asked.

"I don't know, Ted. I certainly hope so," his mother said, as the ambulance moved away from the curb, its siren wailing.

Just as he settled in front of the television, Ted heard a knock at the door. It was his sister, Donna.

"Sorry, but my arms are full, and I couldn't get to my key," she said.

"That's okay," Ted responded. "I needed the exercise."

"Did you guys see them take Mr. Patterson away?" Donna asked.

"Yes, we did, dear. Did you talk with someone across the street?" her mother asked.

"Phil Gordon was there when I walked up. He said Mr. Patterson had a heart attack. Phil couldn't believe how fast the paramedics got there. He said they probably saved Mr. Patterson's life," Donna reported.

"Those paramedics are really something," Ted said. "I'll bet they save a lot of lives."

"I know of several cases already this year," Ted's father said. "When the city council first considered starting a paramedic program, I thought it was too costly. They've changed my mind. I'm glad to pay a few dollars more in property taxes to see Mr. Patterson survive this emergency," he said.

1. What level of government provided the paramedic service needed by Mr. Patterson and the community? Who paid for the service?

_____

_____

_____

2. If Mr. Patterson becomes permanently disabled and unable to work because of his heart attack, what level of government, and specifically what agency, might be involved in providing Mr. Patterson with financial benefits?

_____

_____

_____

CHAPTER 28

THE ROLE
OF
COMPUTERS
IN
BUSINESS
AND
GOVERNMENT

VOCABULARY PRACTICE

Directions: Match the terms in Column *B* with the phrases in Column *A* by writing the letter of the term next to the phrase that best describes that term.

Column A	*Column B*
_____ 1. The field that encompasses computers and their use.	A. data
_____ 2. Manufacturing products under control of a computer.	B. hardware
_____ 3. An item put together from a series of parts.	C. program
_____ 4. Raw facts and figures that are meaningless in and of themselves.	D. information technology
_____ 5. Outputs in the form of pictures or images.	E. random arrangement
_____ 6. A process for representing data about images with numeric values.	F. robot
_____ 7. Computer equipment—electronic and mechanical devices.	G. assembly
_____ 8. An arrangement in which there is no order.	H. CAM
_____ 9. A set of instructions directing the processing of information.	I. graphics
_____ 10. A machine that operates by itself.	J. digitizing

SHORT ANSWER QUESTIONS

Directions: Use your textbook, *The Dynamics of Work,* and your own personal experiences to answer each question in complete sentences.

1. What is the purpose of the record function in an information system?

_____

_____

_____

2. What are the parts of an information system?

_____

_____

_____

3. Why is the storage of data an important capability for an information system?

_____

_____

_____

4. What gives the computer its special value in our modern world?

_____

_____

_____

5. How do computers make it easier to design buildings?

_____

_____

_____

CHAPTER 28 • THE ROLE OF COMPUTERS IN BUSINESS AND GOVERNMENT

SENTENCE COMPLETION

Directions: Using the list below, select the term that best completes each statement. No term is to be used more than once.

record	classify
retrieve	summarize
outputs	communication
information system	documents
data capture	displays

1. A(n) _____ accepts data, processes them, delivers the results, and stores them for later use.

2. Information systems _____ stored data for use.

3. The basic function that achieves input of data is called _____ or _____ .

4. The _____ function makes data useful by determining their nature or type.

5. Totals of different groups of data are produced by the _____ function.

6. Outputs are delivered to users as _____ or _____ .

7. _____ takes place when information is delivered to users.

8. Users receive and use _____ of information systems.

PUT YOURSELF IN THE PICTURE

Directions: Write a brief statement relating this chapter, "The Role of Computers in Business and Government," to your everyday life. Choose a document that you or your family have received that has been generated by a computer. Describe the information system used in the production of the document in terms of its four main parts—input, processing, output, and storage.

_____

_____

_____

_____

_____

_____

_____

_____

_____

_____

_____

_____

_____

_____

CHAPTER 28 • THE ROLE OF COMPUTERS IN BUSINESS AND GOVERNMENT

DYNAMICS AT WORK—CASE 1

Directions: Read the following case carefully. Answer the questions using the information in the case and in Chapter 28.

The family was beginning its day. Mr. Sullivan turned up the volume of the radio so other members of the family could listen. While he showered, Mrs. Sullivan pulled on a robe and straightened the bed. As she worked, she listened carefully to the weather report and the other news.

When the hourly news summary was over, she walked to the bedroom door and called to her son. "Sean, you'd better wear that nylon jacket with the hood. Also put on old pants today. The weatherman says we will probably get thundershowers this afternoon."

In response to Sean's groaning, she continued, "It won't hurt to be prepared. There's no sense in ruining your good jacket if it does rain. Also, with the basketball season approaching, you don't need a cold."

At the breakfast table, Mrs. Sullivan had news for her husband. "Francis, you'd better plan on driving to Grand Boulevard to catch the expressway. The traffic report says there was an accident at the Broadway on-ramp. It may take an hour to clear up the mess."

To both her husband and son, Mrs. Sullivan said, "I think I'll get a turkey for dinner. The radio said our market has a special. We haven't had a turkey in a long time. It will be a celebration. After all, our son doesn't get picked for the varsity basketball team every day. Also, we'll have leftovers for Sean's lunches."

Mr. Sullivan commented, "You're just full of advice and decisions this morning—a walking computer."

Sean joined in, "Mom, you sound like you've been listening to Mr. Shapiro. He teaches my class in decision making and problem solving. He's big on this business of using information to figure out what problems you face. Then you plan actions to avoid the problems. You're always ready for everything."

"That's a good way to be," Mr. Sullivan said, patting his wife's hand. "The idea is to put information to work. You should gather and analyze information before you make decisions. There are decisions you have to make every day. You have to wear something to school. So, your clothes might as well be right for the weather you expect. The same applies for all the decisions you make—personally, in school, and on the job. Information is a tool. It's a mistake not to benefit from use of that tool."

1. Describe the information system Mrs. Sullivan used.

_____

_____

2. What did Mrs. Sullivan do that a computer could not have done?

_____

_____

CHAPTER 28 • THE ROLE OF COMPUTERS IN BUSINESS AND GOVERNMENT

DYNAMICS AT WORK—CASE 2

Directions: Read the following case carefully. Answer the questions using the information in the case and in Chapter 28.

Rosalie was fascinated. This was the first time she had been in a supermarket when no customers were present. The place looked fearfully large and empty. It was just after closing time on her first day of work. Now Rosalie was helping Sheila, the manager, to wind up the day's business. The aisles began to fill up as other employees moved large stacks of merchandise between the displays. Quickly, the workers began to place packages of merchandise on the shelves.

"On a new employee's first day," Sheila explained, "it's usually best to follow me through the closing procedures. That way, you get a chance to look at the whole operation. I'll explain as we go."

Rosalie followed Sheila up a flight of stairs to an office. The office was at the back of the store, over the area where merchandise was received and meat was cut.

"Everything that happens in the store is entered into our information system," Sheila explained. "Our new sales registers are computer terminals. The printed codes on the packages are read right into the computer. The computer then displays the name of the item and its price at the check stand. Here in the office, the computer stores information on how many units of each product we've sold.

"That's only part of our information system," Sheila continued. "Each time a checker begins to use a terminal, the computer keeps track of what happens. I get reports each evening. These tell me how long each check stand was open and what sales were made. So, day by day, we know how many units of each item of merchandise we sell. We also know how many check stands were open and what sales were made during each hour of the day. We can tell how much each checker was able to process."

Rosalie was trying to understand all of this. "That's a lot of information," she said.

A humming noise started suddenly. Rosalie noticed a typewriter-like device that had started to print on a continuous paper form.

"Here comes the first set of reports now," Sheila said. "The information I've told you about so far is only the beginning. We also get comparisons of our operations. Every day, the sales in this store are compared with others in our chain. That means I get information on where we stand in comparison with more than 100 stores. I also get comparisons on our own sales. Today is a Saturday. I'll get figures comparing today's sales with last Saturday's. I'll also get information on total sales for this week and last week. I'll know how we have done so far this year as compared with last year."

"Wow," was all Rosalie could manage.

"Capturing and processing information has become easy with the equipment we have today," Sheila said. "The hard part is to figure out what the information means. Then the even harder part is to plan operations of the store so that we keep improving our performance. Without information from a system like this, we wouldn't know where we stand or where we are going."

"Wow, is there ever a lot to learn," Rosalie said. "I thought I was getting into the food-selling business. Now I see that a company like this is really in the information business as well."

1. Your text says that computers are only a tool to be used by business in processing information. How will Sheila use the computer as a tool in managing the store?

_____

_____

_____

_____

_____

_____

2. Do you believe that all businesses are really information businesses in addition to being producers? Why or why not?

_____

_____

_____

_____

_____

_____

CHAPTER 29

THE
ROLE
AND
VALUE
OF LABOR

VOCABULARY PRACTICE

Directions: Match the terms in Column *B* with the phrases in Column *A* by writing the letter of the term next to the phrase that best describes that term.

Column A

_____ 1. A privileged status gained through length of continuous service.

_____ 2. A process in which both parties in a labor dispute consult a third party to try to settle the dispute.

_____ 3. A work stoppage not approved by the union involved.

_____ 4. Negotiations between an employer and a union.

_____ 5. An organized campaign by union members against the products of an organization being struck.

_____ 6. A state law that outlaws union shops.

_____ 7. A business that hires nonunion workers but requires that they apply for union membership within a specified period of time.

_____ 8. A work stoppage by a body of workers.

Column B

A. collective bargaining
B. strike
C. union shop
D. seniority
E. right-to-work law
F. wildcat strike
G. boycott
H. arbitration

SHORT ANSWER QUESTIONS

Directions: Use your textbook, *The Dynamics of Work,* and your own personal experiences to answer each question in complete sentences.

1. What is the primary function of a labor union?

_____

_____

_____

_____

2. What is the difference between a trade union and an industrial union?

_____

_____

_____

_____

3. What is the basic argument of organized labor in favor of union shops?

_____

_____

_____

4. Why has labor's emphasis switched from wages and salaries to total compensation packages?

_____

_____

_____

5. Why are strikes painful for both sides in a labor dispute?

_____

_____

_____

CHAPTER 29 • THE ROLE AND VALUE OF LABOR

SENTENCE COMPLETION

Directions: Using the list below, select the term that best completes each statement. No term is to be used more than once.

organized labor	strike fund
collective bargaining	grievance
trade union	closed shop
seniority	mediation
union shop	arbitration

1. Members of a(n) _____ are skilled in a particular kind of work.

2. Unlike _____ , the two sides in a labor dispute are not bound by _____ .

3. Under _____ work agreements, new employees must join the union within a specified time.

4. Only union members can be hired in a(n) _____ , which is prohibited by the Taft-Hartley Act.

5. _____ uses _____ to deal with management on behalf of the workers.

6. A(n) _____ is a complaint brought by one or more workers against the employer.

7. Some unions pay benefits to members from a(n) _____ during work stoppages.

8. The workers with the most _____ are usually the last to be laid off.

PUT YOURSELF IN THE PICTURE

Directions: Write a brief statement relating this chapter, "The Role and Value of Labor," to your everyday life. Describe a situation in which you acted as a mediator or arbitrator in a dispute between two friends. Or describe a situation in which a third party helped resolve a dispute in which you were involved. Whichever your role, describe your feelings during the resolution of the dispute.

_____

_____

_____

_____

_____

_____

_____

_____

_____

_____

_____

_____

_____

DYNAMICS OF WORK LOG

Directions: Check off each activity as you complete it. When you have completed the assignments for a unit, write the date of completion in the proper space.

UNIT I.   WORKING

Chapter 1.   You and Business

☐ Vocabulary Practice
☐ Short Answer Questions
☐ Sentence Completion

☐ Put Yourself in the Picture
☐ Dynamics at Work

Chapter 1 completed . . . . ___/___/___

Chapter 2.   The Business System

☐ Vocabulary Practice
☐ Short Answer Questions
☐ Sentence Completion

☐ Put Yourself in the Picture
☐ Dynamics at Work

Chapter 2 completed . . . . ___/___/___

Chapter 3.   Employment: Selecting Your Course

☐ Vocabulary Practice
☐ Short Answer Questions
☐ Sentence Completion

☐ Dynamics at Work
☐ Put Yourself in the Picture

Chapter 3 completed . . . . ___/___/___

Chapter 4.   Preparation for Employment

☐ Vocabulary Practice
☐ Short Answer Questions
☐ Sentence Completion

☐ Put Yourself in the Picture
☐ Putting Some Myths to Rest

Chapter 4 completed . . . . ___/___/___

Chapter 5.   Getting Ready to Apply for Employment

☐ Vocabulary Practice
☐ Short Answer Questions

☐ Sentence Completion
☐ Put Yourself in the Picture

Chapter 5 completed . . . . ___/___/___

Chapter 6.   Applying for Employment

☐ Vocabulary Practice
☐ Short Answer Questions

☐ Sentence Completion
☐ Put Yourself in the Picture

Chapter 6 completed . . . . ___/___/___

Chapter 7.   Getting Along at Work

☐ Vocabulary Practice
☐ Short Answer Questions
☐ Sentence Completion

☐ Dynamics at Work—Case 1
☐ Dyamics at Work—Case 2
☐ Put Yourself in the Picture

Chapter 7 completed . . . . ___/___/___

Chapter 8. Your Rights and Responsibilities on the Job

☐ Vocabulary Practice
☐ Short Answer Questions
☐ Sentence Completion

☐ Put Yourself in the Picture
☐ Dynamics at Work

Chapter 8 completed . . . . ___/___/___

UNIT II.   RESOURCE MANAGEMENT

Chapter 9.   Choosing Your Lifestyle

☐ Vocabulary Practice
☐ Short Answer Questions
☐ Dynamics at Work—Case 1

☐ Dynamics at Work—Case 2
☐ Put Yourself in the Picture

Chapter 9 completed . . . . __/__/__

Chapter 10.   Managing Your Human Resources

☐ Vocabulary Practice
☐ Short Answer Questions

☐ Test Your Creativity
☐ Dynamics at Work

Chapter 10 completed . . . . __/__/__

Chapter 11.   Managing Your Time

☐ Vocabulary Practice
☐ Short Answer Questions

☐ Dynamics at Work
☐ Keeping a Time Log

Chapter 11 completed . . . . __/__/__

Chapter 12.   Managing and Protecting Your Income

☐ Vocabulary Practice
☐ Short Answer Questions

☐ Dynamics at Work
☐ Preparing and Keeping a Budget

Chapter 12 completed . . . . __/__/__

Chapter 13.   Using Financial Services

☐ Vocabulary Practice
☐ Short Answer Questions
☐ Checking Account Transactions

☐ Writing Endorsements
☐ Reconciling a Checking Account

Chapter 13 completed . . . . __/__/__

Chapter 14.   Using Credit to Achieve Financial Goals

☐ Vocabulary Practice
☐ Short Answer Questions

☐ Dynamics at Work

Chapter 14 completed . . . . __/__/__

Chapter 15.   Paying Taxes for Government Services

☐ Vocabulary Practice
☐ Short Answer Questions
☐ Completing a W–4 Form

☐ Completing a 1040EZ Income Tax Return
☐ Completing a 1040A Income Tax Return
☐ Allocating Tax Revenues

Chapter 15 completed . . . . __/__/__

UNIT III.   THE CHANGING WORLD

Chapter 16.   The Meaning of Change

☐ Vocabulary Practice
☐ Short Answer Questions
☐ Sentence Completion

☐ Put Yourself in the Picture
☐ Dynamics at Work—Case 1
☐ Dynamics at Work—Case 2

Chapter 16 completed . . . . __/__/__

Chapter 17. A Process for Dealing with Change

☐ Sentence Completion
☐ Short Answer Questions
☐ Put Yourself in the Picture

☐ Dynamics at Work—Case 1
☐ Dynamics at Work—Case 2

Chapter 17 completed . . . . ___/___/___

Chapter 18. Stress, Conflict, and Pathways to Peace

☐ Vocabulary Practice
☐ Short Answer Questions
☐ Sentence Completion

☐ Put Yourself in the Picture
☐ Dynamics at Work—Case 1
☐ Dynamics at Work—Case 2

Chapter 18 completed . . . . ___/___/___

Chapter 19. Building Problem-Solving and Decision-Making Skills

☐ Vocabulary Practice
☐ Short Answer Questions
☐ Sentence Completion

☐ Put Yourself in the Picture
☐ Dynamics at Work—Case 1
☐ Dynamics at Work—Case 2

Chapter 19 completed . . . . ___/___/___

UNIT IV. PEOPLE AND BUSINESS

Chapter 20. Your Relationships—The Need to Belong

☐ Vocabulary Practice
☐ Malsow's Hierarchy of Needs
☐ Short Answer Questions

☐ Dynamics at Work—Case 1
☐ Dynamics at Work—Case 2
☐ Assessing Behavior in Personal Relationships

Chapter 20 completed . . . . ___/___/___

Chapter 21. Knowing Yourself—A Good Person to Know

☐ Vocabulary Practice
☐ Put Yourself in the Picture
☐ Short Answer Questions
☐ Dynamics at Work
☐ Johari: Window 1—Words That Best Describe
   Myself

☐ Johari: Window 2—Words That Best Describe My Classmate
☐ Johari: Window 3—Words That Best Describe My Classmate
☐ Johari: Window 4—Words That Best Describe My Classmate
☐ Johari: Window 5—As I See Myself
☐ Johari: Window 6—How Others See Me
☐ Johari: Window 7—Discussion

Chapter 21 completed . . . . ___/___/___

Chapter 22. Projecting Your Image

☐ Vocabulary Practice
☐ Short Answer Questions

☐ Personality Inventory
☐ Dynamics at Work

Chapter 22 completed . . . . ___/___/___

Chapter 23. Getting Along in the World of Work

☐ Vocabulary Practice
☐ Short Answer Questions

☐ Dynamics at Work—Case 1
☐ Dynamics at Work—Case 2

Chapter 23 completed . . . . ___/___/___

UNIT V. THE ECONOMIC SYSTEM

Chapter 24. Business–Ideas at Work

☐ Vocabulary Practice
☐ Short Answer Questions
☐ Sentence Completion

☐ Dynamics at Work
☐ Put Yourself in the Picture

Chapter 24 completed . . . . _____/___/_____

Chapter 25. Business and Economics

☐ Vocabulary Practice
☐ Short Answer Questions

☐ Sentence Completion
☐ Dynamics at Work

Chapter 25 completed . . . . _____/___/_____

Chapter 26. The Economic System

☐ Vocabulary Practice
☐ Short Answer Questions
☐ Sentence Completion

☐ Put Yourself in the Picture

Chapter 26 completed . . . . _____/___/_____

Chapter 27. The Role of Business and Government

☐ Vocabulary Practice
☐ Short Answer Questions

☐ Sentence Completion
☐ Dynamics at Work

Chapter 27 completed . . . . _____/___/_____

Chapter 28. The Role of Computers in Business and Government

☐ Vocabulary Practice
☐ Short Answer Questions
☐ Sentence Completion

☐ Put Yourself in the Picture
☐ Dynamics at Work—Case 1
☐ Dynamics at Work—Case 2

Chapter 28 completed . . . . _____/___/_____

Chapter 29. The Role and Value of Labor

☐ Vocabulary Practice
☐ Short Answer Questions

☐ Sentence Completion
☐ Put Yourself in the Picture

Chapter 29 completed . . . . _____/___/_____